To c-

In chist!

♡
S V

MOVE

To C-12 leader,

Chase!

♡

MOVE

THE 4-QUESTION GO-TO-MARKET FRAMEWORK

GTM

SANGRAM VAJRE and BRYAN BROWN

LIONCREST
PUBLISHING

MOVE

The 4-question Go-to-Market Framework

ISBN 978-1-5445-2338-5 *Hardcover*
      978-1-5445-2337-8 *Paperback*
      978-1-5445-2336-1 *Ebook*

CONTENTS

What's your next MOVE?

This book is about to answer that question for every go-to-market leader (VC, CEO, CMO, CRO, CXO) who wants to create a high-performing revenue team to move their organization further faster.

This book is dedicated to YOU, the go-to-market leaders.

That's why all proceeds for 2021 sales of this book are going to support the New Story Charity, an organization that is building a new life for thousands of people in North and Central America so the world can move further faster.

FOREWORD

IT'S TIME TO GET MOVING

By Tim Kopp, Terminus Chairman and CEO

I'M A CEO NOW, BUT I WILL ALWAYS BE A MARKETER at heart. My career was "raised" in marketing. I got my start in B2C with brands like Coca-Cola and P&G, then made the jump to B2B when I took on my first CMO role with WebTrends. From there, I took a bigger jump and joined ExactTarget, where I had the honor of leading a global team of 300 incredible marketers. I was also part of the company's IPO in 2012 and $2.7 billion acquisition by Salesforce.com in 2013.

Then I did something different and began working as an early-stage investor, which led me to Terminus where I'm now CEO and chairman. Of course, I'm glossing over a lot of details, but I was told to keep this "short-ish."

I didn't share all of this to brag about my career. Rather, I just wanted to demonstrate how varied my career has been. However, through all of these different experiences, one omnipresent truth has remained: **the most successful companies are built on strong go-to-market teams.**

Many companies just don't get this. It's shocking to learn how many leaders think they have a marketing problem when they actually have a go-to-market problem, which is exactly what Sangram and Bryan tackle in this book.

In his previous book, Sangram tackled account-based marketing (ABM), but the topic this time is so much bigger. It's about revenue. It's about culture. It's about transformation. Yes, this time it's about movement.

Think of go-to-market as a chain: when customer success, marketing, and sales are all working so well together that you can't tell where one starts and the other stops. The central link to all three of these functions is called *revenue operations* (RevOps), and it serves as the foundation for any high-performing go-to-market team. Getting there isn't just a project. It's a *process* that requires ongoing intentionality.

And to be clear, the buck stops with the CEO. Period. This doesn't rest on the shoulders of your sales leaders or your marketing team. If you're a CEO, read this along with me: Go-to-market is on you!

To be clear, this book is not intended solely for CEOs. Rather, the content and framework provided in these chapters are intended to help CEOs, CMOs, CROs, and all go-to-market leaders who want their companies to succeed.

In this book, you will discover a new way of thinking. A framework to achieve true business transformation, built on what we call "the three Ps" (problem-market fit, product-market fit, and platform-market fit). To get this right, you may have to break some things. Actually, you will *definitely* have to break some things.

Marketing will have to change. Now it's about your company's entire go-to-market approach. You're thinking bigger, and your entire C-suite needs to support your CMO—your change agent—and get on board.

In my opinion, this is the most important movement of the next decade. What's currently out there is, quite frankly, garbage. There's not a single playbook that nails go-to-market. Not a single one.

Until now.

I won't claim that the framework provided in this book is perfect, but I know firsthand what it feels like when companies finally get go-to-market right, and this framework will get you there. So it's time to stop perpetuating junk that doesn't drive outcomes.

In fact, that's the reason why Sangram Vajre and Bryan Brown wrote this book. That's why they did their research, interviewing the gold standard of CEOs, CMOs, CROs, and VCs who are getting go-to-market right. Regardless of your company size, company stage, or industry, if you want to grow, if you want to get your company out of the rut, this book provides the framework you need to do it.

Do you want to transform your company? Then it's time to get moving!

INTRODUCTION

COMPANIES ARE BORN OUT OF DREAMS.

Think about it. Someone had an amazing idea. They dreamed about making something better, newer, easier, more convenient. They dreamed about doing something that had never been done before, and they formed a company to make that dream a reality.

The people they hire along the way buy into the dream and want to help achieve it. Indeed, the thought of realizing that compelling vision energizes them when they come to work every day.

But doing business is messy and unpredictable.

Companies face challenges—competition, changing markets, limited resources, and more—that cause them to underachieve those dreams. There's a relentless, ongoing pressure to grow the company, with employees to pay, customers to serve, and countless other funding needs.

To keep it all going, you have to keep growing.

→

But this stress leads to messy decision making and competing priorities. It becomes harder to answer the question, "What should we do next?" How do you keep a company growing when you don't have clear alignment and don't know exactly which direction to take?

> *How do you keep a company growing*
> *when you don't have clear alignment and don't*
> *know exactly which direction to take?*

As a result, the people who originally bought into it begin feeling a disconnect between what they believed was possible and what they've been consigned to. A divide grows between the vision, hopes, and aspirations that gave birth to the company and the realities of working there. Team members can no longer map their efforts to the company's achievement of the dream. Work begins to lose purpose, and people begin to lose passion. Consequently, it becomes harder to keep people focused and aligned.

Look, even the greatest companies get stuck in this mire of confusion from time to time. Creating a product is easy enough, but building a great company and culture, having the discipline to take a product to market, is vastly more challenging.

Creating a product is easy enough,
but building a great company and culture,
having the discipline to take a product to
market, is vastly more challenging.

The failure to achieve a big dream is a struggle as old as human history.

Before the Wright brothers achieved sustained flight with their motor-operated airplane in 1903, there were many wild and crazy inventors who dreamed up fabulous flying contraptions. Often, they put together talented teams and built those machines, with their heads filled with visions of soaring like an eagle dancing through their heads. And then the day came when they hauled it up to the top of a ramp, or a hill, or God forbid, a sheer cliff on top of a mountain, and they launched it.

Perhaps you've seen some of the old film footage of these failed early endeavors, where the strange winged machine sails down the ramp, briefly leaps into the air, then careens to the ground and breaks into pieces as the distraught inventor and team look on. Every single one of those failed machines started out as the wild-eyed vision of a talented team.

Of course, the original dream wasn't to simply fling a machine off the end of the ramp and somehow keep it from crashing right away. No, the dream of those early inventors was to enable humans to fly like the birds. Successfully launching a plane was only the first big step to making the dream a reality.

For sustained flight to really achieve the vision, they had to figure out how to create vehicles that could reliably take people higher and higher, get them where they wanted to go, and return them to the ground safely every time. Mapping that dream to a practical reality took decades of hard work from talented, hardworking people who took a lot of risks and made smart decisions.

The struggle to achieve reliable air travel gives us a perfect picture of the struggle most companies face. Achieving the dream isn't "one and done." It's an ongoing business transformation from *ideation* to *transition to execution*—also known as "the three Ps" of problem-market fit, product-market fit, and platform-market fit—and somehow, you have to navigate these stages, "the three Ps," without losing momentum and stalling out somewhere along the way.

You have to navigate these stages, "the three Ps," without losing momentum and stalling out somewhere along the way.

You see, it doesn't matter how long an airplane has been flying. At any moment, it's possible for the plane to stall out and take a nosedive into the nearest field if wrong decisions are made. Or to be less dramatic, if the airline company doesn't expand service to the right cities, its growth may stall because it fails to meet customer demand.

This failure happens in the business world all the time. Somewhere along the way—maybe just after launch or maybe after years of hard work—the company fails to fully deliver the company vision to the customer. Leaders don't know which next growth step to take, so the company loses focus, stalls, and gradually down it goes!

But some succeed. What makes the difference? What separates the wild-eyed dreamers from the actual winners?

In a single phrase: *Go-to-market.* More precisely, a high-performing go-to-market (GTM) team and a process for making the dream a reality.

GTM does this by creating a practical path that aligns all of your people with the overarching mission, not just one time but many. It's about ongoing transformation and continued growth. It's about knowing what your next move should be—and your next, and your next, and so on.

> It's about knowing what your next move should be—
> and your next, and your next, and so on.

WHAT IS GO-TO-MARKET?

But what exactly is GTM? GTM is a transformational process for accelerating your path to market where high-performing revenue teams (marketing, sales, and customer success) deliver a connected customer experience and every touchpoint reinforces the brand, values, and vision of your company.

Not a strategy.
Not a project.

Repeatable, scalable, revenue pipeline, at highest ROI.

GTM is a transformational process for accelerating your path to market with high-performing revenue teams delivering a connected customer experience.

Marketing, sales, success & operations and enablement all working together!

Customer is recognized at every touch point. Connected brand experience without all the hand-offs.

In other words, your GTM process connects your company strategy to your customer outcomes, helping customers realize the dream that the company was built on and enjoy the benefits that dream promises to deliver.

> Your GTM process connects your company strategy to your customer outcomes

It might be helpful to visualize the company strategy, customer outcomes, and GTM as three gears that keep your company moving forward, with GTM acting as the connecting gear between the other two. It's these three gears working together that makes extraordinary growth possible.

The role of GTM.

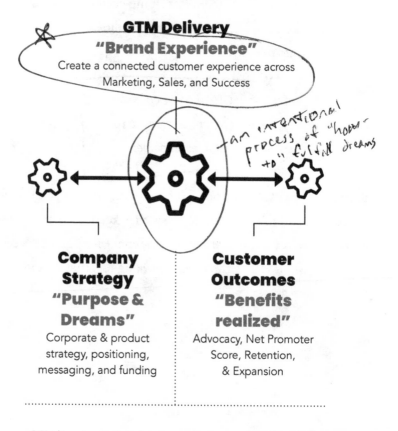

GTM Delivery
"Brand Experience"
Create a connected customer experience across
Marketing, Sales, and Success

I am intentional process of "how" to "fulfill dreams

Company Strategy
"Purpose & Dreams"
Corporate & product
strategy, positioning,
messaging, and funding

Customer Outcomes
"Benefits realized"
Advocacy, Net Promoter
Score, Retention,
& Expansion

GTM lives in service of company strategy and is the vehicle
by which the companies dreams are brought
to its customers.

For most companies, the missing link is that middle gear. They
have a company strategy and they have customers, but they lack a
high-performing GTM function. Consequently, they underper-
form and underachieve, and the dream gets further and further

away from achievable. As a result, customers become increasingly unhappy, and retention declines.

If customer retention is suffering, if customers are complaining more and more, if employee turnover is high, then you *are* underachieving. Maybe there's messiness inside of your business. Sales hit their number, but it wasn't pretty. People are so fatigued that it feels like losing even when they win. Maybe momentum has stalled, so even though everyone is still working hard, no one feels like they're getting ahead.

Whatever the case, you want to know how to course correct and get your company on track, don't you?

Well, it's simple. You just need a clear GTM process to ensure that your company continues to deliver the promise of your vision to both employees and customers. In this book, we intend to give you just that.

But first, let's be crystal clear. Your company strategy is not your GTM strategy. GTM operates in the *service* of your company strategy in order to drive your business forward faster and further—not just once but reliably and repeatedly.

> *Your company strategy is not*
> *your GTM strategy.*

So what does that look like when your GTM operates in the service of your company strategy?

If you're a big online retailer like Amazon, your company strategy is to make your products and services readily accessible on the internet. That is your ongoing mission. Your GTM process, then, is how you plan to achieve some of those elements in the short term.

As you probably recall, Amazon started off with one service: selling books online. Over time, they added other products and services, such as music, videos, groceries, self-publishing services, and more. They entered new markets, improved their processes, and created an increasingly robust platform. Through an ongoing process of transformation and expansion, they continue to open up more ways to provide value to customers and deliver on the promises of their vision. Amazon is truly a well-oiled GTM machine!

After all, what use is your amazing company strategy if you can't deliver it to customers? Or to use our opening story, what use are wings if you can't make them fly, and what good is flying if you can't go higher, faster, and farther more reliably?

WHY IS GO-TO-MARKET SO HARD?

This isn't a guide for creating your company strategy, mission, or vision, and it's not a handbook for building great products. We're here to provide a framework for your GTM process that will help you unlock your potential so you can deliver your unique value proposition to customers and create an enduring company with a sustainable ability to keep growing and scaling.

> *Create an enduring company with a sustainable*
> *ability to keep growing and scaling.*

So many companies struggle with this. Why is it such a problem? We believe it's because leaders don't know what questions to ask. If you want better answers, ask better questions, as the old saying goes.

Adding to the difficulty, GTM is cross-functional and ever changing, so you need to ask those questions over and over again. It's one thing to disrupt the market with a new product. It's another thing altogether to *keep* disrupting the market every few years by reinventing your GTM process. No wonder companies are struggling.

The good news is, you can implement a framework for your GTM strategy by answering just four questions. Here they are, so pay attention! It all comes down to these:

- Whom should we market to?

- What do we need in order to operate effectively?

- When can we scale our business?

- Where can we grow the most?

We can summarize these questions as your market, operations, velocity, and expansion, or MOVE. As it turns out, finding and aligning on the answers to these four questions is a lot more difficult than it seems when you don't have a clear framework for doing so.

We've seen firsthand—at hundreds of B2B companies—how difficult it is to get GTM right. We created the MOVE framework (and wrote this book) out of empathy for CEOs and their GTM teams who are struggling, and we designed it to be simple enough that almost anyone can understand it. The MOVE framework helps you answer these four key questions, providing a maturity matrix that enables you to see where you are now so you can identify and execute your next move. As you grow and evolve, your answers will change, but the questions remain the same.

We didn't create MOVE in a vacuum, nor is it merely a theoretical concept that we want you to test out for us. On the contrary, we've conducted extensive research, interviewed hundreds of business leaders, and surveyed thousands across the B2B world, and one thing has become absolutely clear: no matter the size of your company or the amount of revenue you have, these four questions are *always* key to your GTM strategy.

> **If you can't answer these four questions, you will underperform. Every time. Period.**

Sadly, most companies lack a centralized GTM process. They're not thinking holistically, and there's no one who owns the GTM process. Doing business feels *messy*, and there's a distinct lack of alignment. Often, each team has their own key performance indicators (KPIs) to measure success, but they're all answering different questions with different data and getting different answers, which means they also have misaligned incentives along the customer journey.

For example, the marketing team may be focused entirely on leads, but some of those are the wrong leads (i.e., not ideal customers). Sales is focused on revenue, so they're trying hard to close the deal with some of those bad leads. Customer success is working hard, with increasing frustration, to retain some customers who should never have been sold to in the first place.

> **A telltale sign that your GTM is broken:** *OUGH!*
> **Having to resell to customers during onboarding.**

They're answering the wrong questions from the get-go, getting wrong answers, and creating a circular problem of misalignment that delivers worse and worse results over time. And even when they realize it's not working, companies often try to *make it work* by committing to the misaligned process even harder.

Folks, that's the definition of insanity, and it inevitably leads to growth stall.

If you (1) sell but can't deliver, (2) deliver but can't renew, (3) or renew but can't expand, then there's a growth stall ahead!

This problem is pervasive in the B2B world, where a customer's experience with a brand typically takes many months to develop and involves a complex series of handoffs. This chain of handoffs makes GTM so much harder because somehow all of those different brand experiences must be connected to achieve an overarching and consistent vision with a singular message. If this seems like a daunting task, you're not alone. *MUST HAVE!*

MOVE WORKS!

So here's some good news. The MOVE framework makes the complex simple. It acts as the operator's manual for your GTM process, giving you a precise way to answer those four essential questions, then organize your teams, investment, activities, and KPIs, and put them in motion seamlessly.

MOVE will transform your teams into a well-oiled machine, where all gears turn together to keep your company moving forward in a beautiful way: growing, scaling, and expanding.

> **MOVE will transform your teams into a well-oiled machine.**

Flying higher, faster, and farther more reliably!

Any company that wants to create high-performing GTM revenue teams will benefit from the MOVE framework, because it gives you new ways to get unstuck and keep growing.

We'll show you how to get there. But before we do that, we need to clear up some pervasive and problematic misconceptions about GTM. So let's get started by taking a clarifying look at six truths about GTM that will make your head spin!

Section One

SIX TRUTHS ABOUT GO-TO-MARKET THAT WILL MAKE YOUR HEAD SPIN

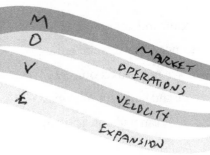

M
O
V
£

MARKET
OPERATIONS
VELOCITY
EXPANSION

WE PROMISED YOU A MOVE FRAMEWORK TO HELP you create a high-performing GTM revenue team, so why are we starting with this "safety spiel" of *six truths*? And what do they have to do with GTM?

Well, it's very simple. As we said in the Introduction, GTM is incredibly hard. Even though it's something that every company needs, leaders have a hard time defining an effective GTM process.

Therefore, in order to provide you with a framework you can implement in your organization, we need to clear the table and sweep off some of the common misconceptions that cause problems.

TRUTH #1: GO-TO-MARKET IS LIKE BUILDING A NEW PRODUCT

When we encourage business leaders to figure out their GTM approach, they often set about fixing it with tremendous enthusiasm, but the way they go about it is all wrong.

They'll bring together their executive team and announce, "Hey, we're having trouble reselling to customers. What we're selling them is not what they were promised. We need to fix our GTM strategy here, so let's plan a two-day offsite and build our strategy as a team. We'll make it really memorable so we can put it on a poster."

Here's the problem. You can't approach GTM as if it were your company strategy, vision, or mission. It's not a trite saying you post on the wall to collect dust. Rather, GTM is an *iterative process* that ensures what you're selling is what you're delivering, and you have to approach it in that way in order to make sure it is always working for you.

> *GTM is an iterative process that ensures what you're selling is what you're delivering.*

Who owns GTM? Which leader is responsible for taking the reins? Our research shows that there is widespread disagreement about this. We asked this question to a thousand business leaders, and here are the responses we got:

But who *should* own it? We're going to say this more than once in the book—it's that important: **GTM belongs to the CEO!**

GTM belongs to the CEO!

When you think about it, there are very few things in a company that a CEO owns. They make sure there's enough money in the bank. They try to ensure that there's a healthy culture and a vision for the future. They also own the company strategy. That's about it.

Fortunately, we find that CEOs often grab hold of GTM and run with it. That's great. However, their approach to GTM isn't always so great. "We need to put our money to work," they say, "so let's rally the troops, and hammer out GTM over the weekend!" In the end, what they typically wind up with after those offsite strategy sessions is some kind of plan to spend money: revenue targets for sales, hiring targets, a bigger marketing budget, and so on. They also usually tweak the mission statement and core values.

We want to be clear about this, so we're going to say it again: GTM is not a strategy, mission, or vision, and you can't approach it in that way. It's an *iterative process* that helps you achieve your corporate strategy, and it must be approached accordingly.

GTM is not a strategy, mission, or vision but an iterative process that helps you achieve your corporate strategy.

For GTM to be iterative, it must become part of the rhythm of how you do business. It must be tweaked constantly as your company matures, grows, and evolves. As Scott Brinker, current

Vice-President of Platform Ecosystem at HubSpot, points out, "Go-to-market is not a project." Well said! A project is a temporary work effort with a clear start and end date, but an iterative process like GTM must continue.

It might be helpful to follow HubSpot CEO Brian Halligan's advice and treat GTM like a *product*. With a product, you get feedback and iterate on it over time. The latest Apple iPhone doesn't bear much resemblance to the iPhone 3GS released in 2007. Why? Because the company keeps iterating on it, using customer feedback and other data to make improvements over time.

GTM is not a project.
Treat GTM like a product.

Heck, to use our earlier example, the commercial airplanes that fly all over the world bear almost no resemblance to the Wright brothers' first plane. Generations of company leaders have worked hard to constantly improve the design and processes around air travel in order to deliver on the original promise of sustained powered flight.

Why is this distinction important? Because if you treat GTM like a product, then you're more likely to keep investing in it. You'll keep making it better, enhancing it, and implementing updates. It'll become a living, breathing process that keeps your company moving forward to the next best opportunity.

TRUTH #2: REVENUE TEAM HAS
A NEW ROOMMATE

This is an easy mistake to make. If you met a guy whose official job title was President of Snake-Handling, you'd assume that his job had something to do with handling snakes, wouldn't you? That would be a reasonable conclusion, and no one would fault you for it. Well, if we call this process GTM, then it must be about marketing. It's right there in the name: *market*. It has to be about marketing!

Nope. GTM certainly *involves* your marketing team, but it's not a marketing process. However, this mistake has led many companies to limit GTM solely to their product launches. That's only one small piece of a more complex puzzle.

If you read our previous book, *ABM Is B2B*, you might view GTM as simply an extension of account-based marketing. In *ABM Is B2B*, we presented the TEAM framework: *target, engage, activate*, and *measure*. That full-on strategy was intended to bring your marketing and sales teams together using the ABM mindset.

In case you *didn't* read our previous book, allow us to clarify. ABM is about your marketing and sales teams working together to pick relevant accounts that they want to go after.

But now, with the addition of the GTM process, <u>marketing and</u> sales have a new roommate.

also about

Who is this new roommate? **Customer success.**

Yes, the core of GTM is about creating high-performing revenue teams that connect marketing, sales, *and* customer success. You have to bring all three to the table because GTM focuses on the entire revenue stream, from new acquisition to pipeline velocity, expansion, upsell, cross-sell, and more.

GTM isn't just a marketing *thing*;
it's a *high-performing revenue thing*.

Put another way, it's not merely the commonplace "going to market," which is what a lot of companies do. They approach the marketing team and say, "Hey, figure out our marketing strategy." On the contrary, in GTM, the whole company is going to market, so everyone needs to get involved.

GTM is about creating high-performing
revenue teams that connect marketing, sales,
and customer success.

Sorry to break the news to you, but if you're struggling to bring your marketing and sales teams together, GTM is only going to make things a heck of a lot more difficult because now you're pulling in a third function: customer success.

If marketing and sales can't work together well, adding customer success into the fray isn't going to fix anything. Think of it this way: A soccer team comprised of players who can't coordinate with one another won't do any better by adding a brand-new player who also can't coordinate well. Teach the existing team members to play well together and then you can add a new player.

TRUTH #3: SMALL IS THE NEW BIG

When most companies are about to go out into the marketplace, they sit down and excitedly talk about how big of a market they're going after.

"Should we go after this $5 billion market? We could potentially reach 100,000 people if we capture it!"

The sheer size of the market entices them. In reality, they're never going to sell to every customer in that $5 billion market. They're aiming way too broadly. It's like trying to wash your car with a water balloon. You'll never get the whole thing wet.

Most businesses will be far better served by narrowing their focus from total addressable market (TAM) to total *relevant* market

(TRM). In other words, instead of trying to reach every possible customer in the biggest market, focus on the customers that are most relevant for the product you have today in the market that is the most relevant for you today. Try to reach those relevant customers in a way that will make them happy, loyal, and willing to pay in order to consume more products and services.

> *Focus on the customers that are most relevant*
> *for the product you have today.*

We'll go into more detail on this later, but you can think of it this way: As Nick Mehta, CEO of Gainsight, put it, "If you're selling hamburgers, it makes sense to put a hamburger stand on every street corner where there's foot traffic, but that model doesn't work for B2B."

In the B2B world, you can't just keep hiring salespeople and throwing them into the market until you reach everyone. After all, you might have to go upmarket, downmarket, verticalize, or adopt persona-based customer segments—each of which requires different GTM alignment. You might have to add products or shift to a completely different market. In a B2B environment, you have to be a lot more agile. Therefore, instead of going really big and focusing on TAM, trying to reach everyone, go small and direct your efforts to your TRM.

Instead of going really big,
go small and direct your efforts to your
total relevant market (TRM).

[rough] If you start big, you're going to underserve all your customers. You won't know which direction to take your product or whom you're serving, and you won't have enough money to keep trying to figure it out. By starting small, focusing on your most relevant customers based on the product fit you have today, you can get it right and then punch out of that box into another bigger box when you're ready.

Too many entrepreneurs create a huge TAM for their pitch deck, aiming as big as possible, in order to raise money, and that's fine. However, once you raise the money and get ready to work, start with the smallest and most relevant slice of the market. Attack that first, do well, and then you can expand your total relevant market and keep growing.

TRUTH #4: REVOPS IS THE
NEW GROWTH LEVER

Many companies lack a single source of truth—it's a common problem. You've probably experienced this. You're in a meeting with a marketing leader, a sales leader, and a customer success leader, and somehow you have to make a decision about what is and isn't working. But marketing, sales, and customer success all have their own data, and you spend twenty, thirty, forty minutes (or more) debating whose numbers are right.

Quite frankly, questions about the business can't be answered by isolated departments.

> *Questions about a business can't be answered by isolated departments.*

"What does our churn look like? Where are we selling the most? Do we have the right leads? Do we have the right accounts?"

Without standardized, accurate, and holistic data, how can you determine any of these things? Instead of making decisions, you end up batting opinions around the room and struggling to get anywhere.

This is a clear indication that you need a RevOps team. RevOps is a new function that very few organizations have embraced, but we believe it's going to be mission critical for creating effective GTM processes.

Revenue Operations

The RevOps team solves the problem of competing and misaligned teams by becoming the "truth teller" of your organization.

Since they have no emotional attachment to any particular area, they are able to look objectively at what's working and not working in the organization. For example, at Terminus, the head of RevOps takes the first fifteen minutes of every meeting to share a GTM scorecard that shows each of the teams how the company is doing (we will share GTM scorecards later in the book).

She reports to our CFO, though in other companies, the head of RevOps might report to the CEO or COO. The point is to give RevOps full autonomy and independence from the marketing, sales, and customer success teams so they can report the numbers without bias or emotion.

In our experience, this works very well because the numbers are clear and no longer a matter of opinion. Teams can focus on solutions to problems instead of fighting over their own version of the truth.

It's a game changer. We believe RevOps is the new growth lever, allowing you to make accurate decisions and grow your organization faster. We will discuss RevOps in greater detail when we dive into the O of the MOVE framework (aka operations), including which KPI your RevOps team needs to focus on at each stage of your business.

TRUTH #5: RETENTION IS THE NEW ACQUISITION

Most B2B marketers focus their attention on the top of the sales funnel, trusting that the sales and customer success teams will assiduously support the middle and bottom of the funnel. But we're approaching a time when every marketer's world is going to be flipped upside down as their primary KPI shifts to customer lifetime value (CLV).

"flip the funnel"

Every marketer's world is going to be
flipped upside down as their primary KPI shifts
to customer lifetime value (CLV).

In this new era, as budgets get tightened at the top of the funnel, the main goal of marketing teams will now be on maintaining and growing their existing customer base.

Let's look at how this works and why it matters so much. We'll use two theoretical companies. We could give them clever names, but let's just call them Company A and Company B.

Company A and Company B are competitors, each bringing in roughly the same amount of revenue each quarter. As the graphic below makes clear, Company A is churning one $500 customer each quarter, while Company B churns three. At the end of the year, Company A winds up with five times the annual recurring revenue (ARR) simply by doing a little better with customer retention. *we live here!*

The math here is elementary-level stuff: low churn rate = higher ARR.

And you know what's even better than a low churn rate? A negative churn rate! That doesn't mean customers can't churn. Rather, it means your built-in revenue is growing faster than your churn rate through upselling, cross-selling, and expansion.

According to Invesp, it's five times more expensive to acquire a new customer than to retain one, so marketing teams are stunting their overall revenue growth when they focus on the top of the funnel instead of their customer base.[1]

> It's five times more expensive to acquire
> a new customer than to retain one.

---

[1] Khalid Saleh, "Customer Acquisition vs. Retention Costs—Statistics and Trends," Invesp, [insert access date], https://www.invespcro.com/blog/customer-acquisition
-retention/.

Company A

Churns 1 Customer Per Quarter

	1Q	2Q	3Q	4Q	Year End
Starting Arr	$10,000	$10,500	$12,000	$12,500	
New Arr	$1,000	$2,000	$1,000	$3,000	$7,000
Churn Arr	$500	$500	$500	$500	$2,000
Ending Arr	$10,500	$12,000	$12,500	$15,000	$15,000
New Net Arr	$500	$1500	$500	$2,500	$5,000

Company A and Company B (B-Next slide) are very comparable competitors. They're both bringing in exactly the same amount of revenue every quarter. Neither are perfect, but Company A is churning one $500 customer every quarter while Company B is churning three. Company A ended the year with 5x the ARR just by doing a little bit better on their customer retention.

Company B

Churns 3 Customer Per Quarter

	1Q	2Q	3Q	4Q	Year End
Starting Arr	$10,000	$9,500	$10,000	$9,500	
New Arr	$1,000	$2,000	$1,000	$3,000	$7,000
Churn Arr	$1,500	$1,500	$1,500	$1,500	$6,000
Ending Arr	$9,500	$10,000	$9,500	$11,000	$11,000
New Net Arr	-$500	$500	-$500	$1,500	$1,000

Even better than low churn rate is negative net churn, which means that not only are you maintaining your recurring revenue, but you're expanding it. That doesn't mean that customers can't churn—it just means that your built in revenue is growing faster than it's churning by up sell, cross-sell or expansions programs.

When an economic storm hits, like the one that followed in the wake of COVID-19, the CMOs who focus on maintaining and growing their CLV are going to weather the storm a whole lot better than those who stay focused on top-line growth.

[handwritten: US !!!]

[handwritten: Customer Lifetime Value]

TRUTH #6: FLYWHEELS ARE THE NEW FUNNELS

Contrary to popular opinion, you don't need a *lead* funnel. Most companies have them. Many companies love them, but the ugly truth about a lead funnel is that, according to Forrester, less than 1 percent of those leads will come out of the other end of that funnel as loyal customers. Those are terrible results, and you don't become more efficient by cramming even more leads into the top of the funnel.

> *Less than 1 percent of those leads will come out of the other end of that funnel as loyal customers.*

We recommend tossing that lead funnel right in the garbage and getting yourself a *revenue flywheel* instead. Shift your focus from simply driving lead volume to efficient and effective revenue growth, where the goal is to progress opportunities with accounts that are a good fit. It's quality over quantity, and every stage of the account life cycle has roughly equal weight.

[handwritten: HUGE NUGGET !!!]

Practically speaking, it means when you bring a customer in the door the first time, you move them through a process that sets them up for long-term success and happiness with your brand so they will come back around for more products, services, and value over time. As they come back around, you're also creating new use cases, new personas, more teams and departments, more products and services. In other words, it's a focus on full-revenue-cycle thinking.

We recommend envisioning it as a flywheel rather than a funnel because a flywheel suggests a constantly repeating cycle that builds on itself over time in order to gain momentum.

Your funnel is a wasteful churn machine. You don't need a faster funnel because you'll just churn faster.

A flywheel is about creating efficient circular movement through customer retention. A customer comes through your door (literally or metaphorically), then they come back through your door a year later, and a year later, and a year later. That's what should be happening, not just cramming leads into the top of a funnel.

p34, image →

GTM
PROCESS

MARKETING

SALES

GO-TO-MARKET

CUSTOMER SUCCESS

Six Truths About GTM That Will Make Your Head Spin

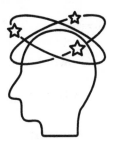

Go-to-Market Is Like Building a New Product.

Revenue Team Has a New Roommate:
Customer Success

Small Is the New Big (focus on TRM not TAM).

RevOps Is the New Growth Lever.

Retention Is the New Acquisition.

Flywheels Are the New Funnels

The purpose of sharing these six truths was to set the table so we're all starting from the same place as we dive into our GTM framework. Before we move on, it might be helpful to recap these truths so you can keep them in mind as we delve into the MOVE framework.

- ▸ GTM Is Like Building a New Product.

- ▸ Revenue Team Has a New Roommate: Customer Success.

- ▸ Small Is the New Big (focus on TRM, not TAM).

- ▸ RevOps Is the New Growth Lever.

- ▸ Retention Is the New Acquisition.

- ▸ Flywheels Are the New Funnels

As we said before, the big difference between companies that experience real growth and companies that only dream of growth comes down to one thing: creating an effective GTM process with high-performing revenue teams. Instead of marketing, sales, and customer success operating in their individual silos, each with its own focus, they work together with a focus on revenue. Hopefully, that is clear to you now.

Indeed, knocking down the silos and bringing your marketing, sales, and customer success teams together is such an integral part of GTM that from this point on, we're just going to refer to this combination as your *revenue team*. When we talk about the GTM process, we're talking about the MOVE framework, and when we talk about revenue teams, we're talking about marketing, sales, and customer success.

Is that clear? Good.

> *When we talk about revenue teams,*
> *we're talking about marketing, sales,*
> *and customer success.*

So, to use our airplane metaphor, we've clarified some key aspects of flight travel so you can avoid common misconceptions that will keep your plane from flying higher, farther, and faster. Now we're ready to get your plane up in the air and really make it soar with the MOVE framework.

Check out themovebook.com to download assessment, templates, and workbooks that will help you turn your GTM silos into a high-performing revenue team.

Idea for a training luncheon

Section Two

NAVIGATING THE GO-TO-MARKET MATURITY CURVE

Business Transformation from Ideation to Execution

LET'S SUPPOSE WE WERE GIVING YOU INSTRUCtions for how to fly your plane higher, farther, and faster more reliably. Our advice would vary depending on where you are in the lifetime of your airplane company, wouldn't it? Trying to get your flying machine off the end of the ramp and into the air for the first time is a very different process from trying to tweak your design so your air service can reach more cities.

In a similar way, in order to make your iterative GTM process work for you, you have to figure out the best way to implement it in your organization based on the stage of your business. To do that, you need to understand the GTM maturity curve so you can figure out where you are (and where you're going).

> *Understand the GTM maturity curve so*
> *you can figure out where you are*
> *(and where you're going).*

This is the place where many companies experience complete and utter *paralysis*. They try to implement a GTM process, but they find themselves struggling far more than they thought they would. We've talked to CEOs of public companies who have struggled with GTM for over a decade, and they've finally come to the conclusion that they're just no good at it.

"I don't know what's wrong with us," they say. "I've had marketing, sales, and customer success hammering away at this for a long time, and we just can't seem to get it right."

We've met team members of companies who are having trouble with GTM and assume they must lack the skill or ability to pull it off. In reality, they just need a way to assess their company's maturity so they can figure out where they are on the maturity curve and understand how it impacts the GTM transformation process.

Every company wants to grow, but in order to do so, you have to navigate several stages of business transformation. In this chapter, we'll explain each of these stages and help you figure out where you are. That way, you can figure out what kind of transformation your business needs to go through in order to get unstuck and progress toward the next stage.

As it turns out, there are three stages of GTM business transformation (and their corresponding three Ps):

SUPER IMPORTANT!
The three stages and three Ps of
GTM business transformation!

- **Ideation (problem-market fit):** lead-focused, sales-led, inefficient growth.

- **Transition (product-market fit):** account-focused, sales + marketing aligned, efficient growth.

- **Execution (platform-market fit):** customer-focused, integrated revenue team (marketing, sales, and customer success), efficient growth at scale.

Let's look at each of these stages and discuss how you implement business transformation at each of them.

As we do that, keep one thing in mind: Revenue is *not* the material indicator of your current stage. You can have $20 million in revenue and still be at the *ideation* stage, figuring things out, or you might race through to the transition stage with only $8 million in revenue.

> *Revenue is not the material indicator*
> *of your current stage.*

Similarly, you can have $150 million in revenue and still be in the *transition* stage, with plenty of room to grow, while another company navigates to the *execution* stage with much less revenue in order to keep growing. It all depends on the dynamics of your industry, market, category, and offering.

Last, companies in the execution stage, especially large global and complex companies, often operate in multiple business stages at the same time. Think of Amazon. In 2006, when their flagship e-commerce platform was already squarely in the *execution* stage, they publicly launched Amazon Web Services, which had a completely different target market, in the *ideation* stage. Thus, Amazon had two completely different businesses, sharing a brand and core technology, requiring two different GTM processes.

Here's a brief overview of each stage.

In the **ideation stage**, you don't have a fully developed product yet. Instead, you are working hard to make sure that the problem your product is meant to solve is big enough (and the market is big enough) to achieve success.

> *In the ideation stage, you don't have a fully developed product yet, and that's okay!*

Think about a brand-new company that is trying to march boldly into the world with their amazing new product. How do they typically find the right market to enter? They look at the size of the market, right?

"Hey, this is a $5 billion market! Think about all of the money we could make if we captured it. Can we do it? Does our solution fit the problem well enough to make an impact?"

That's the primary focus at this stage: *problem-market fit.*

In other words, if you're trying to develop an amazing new toaster with AI capabilities, you'd better make sure the market needs an amazing new toaster with AI capabilities. More specifically, you'd better make sure the market needs *your* toaster.

The second stage of business transformation is what we call the **transition stage**, and at this stage, most businesses are focused on *product-market fit.*

They know they need a set number of people buying their product or service, and by this point, they've had enough development and iterations that they've got the right product for the right market.

You've got the right product for the right market.

So you've worked hard on your fancy new AI toaster, and you're confident that it will provide the best solution for your ideal customer's needs. Now the sales team needs a repeatable and scalable process so they can sell more of the product and claim an ever-bigger piece of the market.

The third and final stage of business transformation is the **execution stage**, which is about *platform-market fit*.

You can't become the next HubSpot or Salesforce—or, for that matter, Terminus—without having a platform that fits your market. In other words, you have to go beyond the idea of a single product to become a multiproduct company, and it's all of those products together that comprise your company's platform.

You have to go beyond the idea of a single product
to become a multiproduct company.

You've grown beyond direct sales in a single market to new regions and new locations. Your persona has developed as your market continues to grow bigger and your platform becomes more diverse.

You're no longer just selling a fancy chrome-plated toaster with AI capabilities. You've now got a whole suite of cutting-edge appliances that can utterly transform the kitchen experience for your ideal customer.

So as you grow through the three stages of GTM transformation, your focus shifts from *problem* to *product* to *platform*.

By the time you arrive at the execution stage, you should already have a solid understanding of how your product fits in the market so you can now acquire or build new products, expand into new markets, and continue to evolve for greater and greater revenue.

That's a basic overview of the three stages and three Ps of GTM business transformation, but now let's dive deeper. Our goal is to help you understand how you will apply the MOVE framework (answering the four key questions) at each of these stages.

In order to get the big picture, we will examine this at the CEO level, but the impacts will be felt by every leader throughout your organization. The CEO has the best overall understanding of where the business is at today, so they will play the most vital role in making sure that the organization adopts the right GTM approach for whichever stage they're at. They will then know when it's time to move to the next stage.

Of course, you don't know where you should be in the MOVE framework until you know where you already are. You have to know what you *need now* in order to take the next big step forward as an organization. We've put together an assessment you can use to help you identify *exactly* where you are on the GTM maturity curve so you can begin to map the way forward. You'll find it near the end of the book.

For now, let's dive deeper into the stages of the GTM maturity curve. Here's a graphic that will help you wrap your head around it.

The Three Stages and the 3Ps of GTM Business Transformation

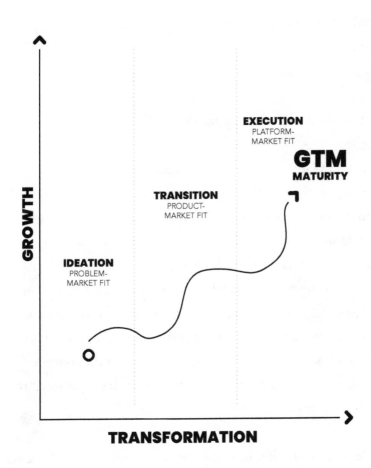

You'll notice on the graph that the growth line isn't linear. Instead, it has a number of dips as it moves from one stage to the next. The key to sustained growth is to catch your company at the right point along this growth line. If you don't, you could wind up on a slippery slope. Remember the flying contraption careening to the ground? This is where it's most likely to happen.

Why do so many companies fail to transform their GTM in time?

It usually goes something like this.

The CEO hires a sales leader who builds a team and starts to see wins, but they get those wins on heroics alone. In other words, they propel themselves into the market and sell ahead using vision and imagination, building consensus with their new customers about historical solutions that have failed to address their problem. They iterate that sales pitch daily, testing and trying new buyer types. The product changes weekly, so customers are excited about the possibilities and buy into it, even before the product is fully "there." Sales starts to hit the numbers, and as the company gets closer to figuring out the problem they are trying to solve, they hit their stride.

But eventually, they reach the end of the runway. Why? Because they can't scale without a process and repeatability, and you can't hire heroics. Sales may be able to hit the numbers for a few more quarters, but eventually, the company will stall and get stuck. To prevent that, they have to transform the way they work—the way they market, sell, and service—before the dip.

The very things you need in order to get off the ground will bring you crashing back down to the ground if you don't change them in time.

So whose job is it to see two quarters ahead? Whose job is it to notice that the executive team isn't aligned or is aligned incorrectly for the next stage of growth? Whose job is it to realize that the KPIs they are using are not what they need to drive the business forward and align their teams? Or that the ability to win with heroics is the very thing that will keep them from hitting the next growth stage? *(connect to these pain points)*

C12 to help

Who else can it be but the CEO? The CEO alone must see ahead and push transformation for the next stage. Once you've figured out problem-market fit, you either transform and grow or stay and get stuck. The same hold true for the other two stages of transformation.

Ideation Stage: Problem-Market Fit

In the ideation stage, you're focused on the problem that your product or service is intended to solve. There are many questions that need to be answered, but they fall into two basic categories:

- Are you creating a solution that fits the market right now?

- Is the market big enough for your solution?

Your focus in this stage is on leads, so your team will typically be led by sales. We might even call this the lead-generation stage, since that is how your GTM team will be working to create volume.

It's a sales-led effort, with people making a lot of outbound calls, but it's inefficient growth. You're very reactive at this stage. No company can afford to park too long at this stage in the maturity curve. Because of inefficient growth and the law of big numbers, it won't take long before your company's growth begins to stall.

Remember our amazing flying machine? When it first comes off the end of the ramp (or the edge of the cliff), it is in a very precarious place. If it doesn't get some lift right away, it's going to flop down onto the ground and break into pieces. The same goes for a company in the ideation stage.

Since your focus is on leads, you will build GTM at this stage in terms of volume: lists, events, digital ads, inbound and outbound, calls and demos.

⟶

From Ideation to Transition

Let's be clear, it's not wrong to be at any particular stage of business maturity. If you're in the ideation stage, it's not bad that you're focused on leads. You're still figuring out your *total addressable market* (TAM). You're still trying to solve a problem in the market in the right way, and you have to make sure it's a big enough problem to create a successful business.

You can't start picking target accounts because you don't know what "ideal" looks like yet.

⟶

At this point, you *need* sales volume and a whole lot of leads. You *need* your reps calling, calling, and calling some more because every time they reach out to an account, they're going to learn a little more about the problem-market fit. As they learn, that knowledge will come back into the company and help you clarify what your ideal customer looks like.

However, at some point during the ideation stage, the volume of leads starts to become untenable because you need more and more of them as the board keeps increasing your revenue number. Your approach becomes increasingly inefficient, and you struggle to retain some of your customers, especially those who were not ideal to begin with. It costs more and more to keep your volume up, and as the numbers rise, you eventually reach a peak where you realize that your way of doing business simply won't get you to the next level of growth.

telltale signs of needed change

(Your approach becomes increasingly inefficient, and you struggle to retain some of your customers.)

That's when you know it's time to make a transition because this is where stalling occurs. If you linger, your plane is going down.

To get to the next stage, you need to start building a different GTM team, with leaders focused on different metrics. They will shift from funnel conversions and cost-per-lead to pipeline coverage, customer acquisition cost, gross revenue retention all broken out by segment performance.

In the ideation stage, marketing and sales aren't fully aligned because they're still learning. Each team is doing its own thing, but as you transition to the next stage, they must come together and start working toward the same goals, numbers, and metrics, all aligned around *segmentation*, delivering your offering or service to relevant (and approachable) groups.

Here's the tricky part. You have to recognize *early* when it's time to make this change because it takes a while to transform. As we said, if you stay in the ideation stage too long, your company is going to stall—and possibly crash and burn—and by the time you realize you're stalling out, it might be too late.

> *By the time you realize you're stalling out,*
> *it might be too late.*

There are a number of reasons why some companies never get beyond this stage.

Any of the following can prevent you from leaving *ideation* and entering the *transition* stage:

- You're trying to scale but haven't found the ideal customer for your product.

- Heavy discounting and renewing down: your key use case is getting commoditized.

- Your brand and positioning are weak, leading to poor demand and win rates.

- There's no primary reason for churn, so there's no clear resolution.

- You have no common enemy, and therefore, you have no direction.

- Customers are unsure of the ROI of your product when renewal time approaches.

- What you sell is not what you deliver.

- You have a lack of repeatability in your sales team— relying on heroics of a few to hit plan.

If you're struggling to get out of the ideation stage, go through this list and see if you can identify which of these issues are present in your company at the moment. You will have to address them now before you can gain some altitude and move onward and upward.

Let's make this transition as crystal clear as possible. What are the clear indicators that it's time to transform? And what are the benefits of making the change?

The answer to these questions is simple.

Once you're confident that you have the right product in the right market for the right customer (those who see the ROI of your solution and renew), then it's probably time to start making the change.

Your focus is now about getting efficient growth, so you need to introduce segmentation and align your teams around a set of accounts that they can sell to in order to achieve it.

Transition Stage: Product-Market Fit

Once you have a product that customers believe in and renew on, you're at the transition stage, where your marketing and sales teams are getting aligned on what needs to happen. Some repeatable processes have been put in place, and you've become proactive about whom you're going after.

> *Once you have a product that customers believe in and renew on, you're at the transition stage.*

Your flying contraption can take off and land safely and reliably. Now you just need to keep building and improving the plane and processes so you can fulfill that dream of reliably transporting passengers from city to city.

Bear in mind, even when you enter this stage, you may continue to suffer from poor retention as a result of the many and varied kinds of customers you sold to during the ideation stage.

That's why measuring performance by segment is critical to knowing which customers to go after and which to abandon.

At this stage, you may also explore the possibility of expansion, but these efforts remain decentralized. After all, you're still figuring things out, even though you now have a great product-market fit. This can be called the accounts stage because you're no longer just chasing leads. You have target customers that you're pursuing, and growth has become more efficient.

It's a great place to be, and quite frankly, some companies get here and never leave. However, staying too long exposes your business to the risk of being disrupted or commoditized—and the corresponding decrease in average deal size.

Since your focus now is on accounts, your GTM process will focus on quality acquisition by design using segmentation: named accounts and tiers, prescriptive plays, better fit, happier customers, higher annual contract value.

From Transition to Execution

To make the final majestic leap from the transition stage to the execution stage, you have to shift from trying to solely grow your business using new bookings to growing your business from an existing customer base.

Your existing customer base will sow the seeds for new customers.

At this point, you need to create customer segments, not just net new account segments, and your metrics are going to focus on customer lifetime value (CLV), net revenue retention (NRR), and multiproduct adoption (MPA) as you expand into new categories, create new solutions, and acquire new companies.

You're building a *much* bigger business.

The flying machine has become a fleet of airplanes transporting more people to more cities with an increasing variety of experiences for travelers.

Any of the following can prevent you from leaving the transition stage and entering the execution stage:

- You've continued to focus on a single product because you have weak vision.

- You've underinvested in the distribution required for future revenue growth.

- You have only one way to hit your number, and there's a lack of predictability.

- Your second or third products are really just features of the first, which is a sign of a weak product strategy.

- Your second or third products aren't taking flight (but should be) due to poor incentive structures or enablement across your revenue teams.

- You're trying to compete on multiple fronts while dominating none.

- Everyone is working, but no one is winning: clear lack of executive alignment.

- Teams don't understand their role in executing the strategy, and they're ill-equipped to say no to anything.

Execution Stage: Platform-Market Fit

Once you have multiple products or services in the market with integrated RevOps (which we'll discuss later), you're at the platform-market stage. You're now making opportunistic, long-range moves with your money because you are focused on expanding growth potential.

There's almost no limit to the number of places your airplanes can travel and almost no limit to the number of travelers you can carry. You can spread your fleet as far and wide as your team and GTM will take you.

At this point, you should be centralizing your processes.

Marketing, sales, and customer success should now be working together like a highly trained flight crew.

They're a revenue-focused GTM team creating efficient growth at scale.

Your focus now is on long-term customers, so your GTM process will be about long-term growth ability. This means relevant accounts become lifetime customers with expansive value.

Relevant accounts become
lifetime customers with
expansive value.

By the time you reach the execution stage (even more so if you are a public company or hope to become one soon), you should have a GTM process that delivers both repeatably and predictably, as noted in the bottom two boxes of this helpful chart from Edison Partners.

Now, one thing to keep in mind. Just because you transition to a new stage doesn't mean you abandon everything that came before. For example, just because your focus is no longer on leads once you've grown into the transition and execution stages doesn't mean you won't still have revenue from lead growth.

Just because you're deep into the execution stage doesn't mean you won't still target new accounts. Rather, you're building a team that can focus on the *key approach of your current stage* so you continue to grow.

GO TO MARKET
Maturity Model

UNDEFINED

Company strategy
may exist, but
go-to-market
strategy does not.

The company
operates in disorder.

Business
performance
is inconsistent
and go-to-market
functions are unable
to repeat successes
consistently.

DEFINED

Company and
go-to-market
strategies exist,
but are not actively
in play and serving
as the necessary
glue across the
organization.

REPEATABLE

Consistent
measurement,
execution and
results across
go-to-market
initiatives and
supporting
functions.

MANAGED

Company and
go-to-market
strategies are
defined, aligned
and reasonably
operationalized.

Respective
go-to-market
functions have
measurable
initiatives to which
they are held
accountable.

PREDICTABLE

Execution and results
are not only repeatable,
but forecasting of the
business is predictable.
A strong indicator of
predictability: the
company has hit or
exceeded plan (across the
most critical go-to-market
and growth metrics) for
three straight quarters.

**If you want to keep growing,
you *must* navigate the maturity
curve of GTM transformation.**

To do that, you first have to figure out where you are now. Then you can begin to figure out what your next step needs to be.

Orchestrating that next move is what the MOVE framework is all about. By answering the four questions of the MOVE framework, you can figure out how to get from *ideation* to *transition* to *execution*. You can grow your single airplane into a fleet of airplanes traveling to more places around the world and creating a better experience for passengers.

In the next chapter, we will give you that framework.

**Check out themovebook.com to download
assessment, templates, and workbooks
that will help you turn your GTM silos into
a high-performing revenue team.**

Section Three

THE MOVE
FRAMEWORK

*Market, Operations, Velocity,
and Expansion*

AT THIS POINT, YOU PROBABLY HAVE QUITE A FEW
questions about GTM. Maybe it still seems fairly complicated, but
we're about to give you a framework that is really going to make
it easy for you to wrap your head around GTM.

It all comes down to four simple questions. We mentioned them
in the Introduction, but now we're going to dive deeply into each
of them.

The four questions of the MOVE framework:

- *Whom* should we market to? (**M**arket)

- *What* do we need to operate effectively? (**O**perations)

- *When* can we scale our business? (**V**elocity)

- *Where* can we grow the most? (**E**xpansion)

**The MOVE framework of
GTM transformation = Market +
Operations + Velocity + Expansion**

Regardless of the size of your company, your industry, or the nature of your products and services, if you can answer these four questions well, you will be able to orchestrate your next move with confidence.

Think about it. Answering just four questions will reveal the most amazing growth opportunity for your company so you can orchestrate your next move. You don't have to go racing off in twenty different directions.

All you have to do is figure out who, what, when, and where.

If only everything in life were so simple.

Answering just four questions
will reveal the most amazing growth
opportunity for your company.

So how do you answer these questions? Let's summarize the process.

First, you have to figure out whom you're going to **market** to. That's the obvious starting point.

Once you've selected a relevant market, you have to make sure you have the **operations** in place to effectively go after your chosen market.

This is where RevOps comes into play: aligning the right people with the right repeatable processes driven by the right data, tech, and metrics to shepherd you into your chosen market and monitor things as you go. RevOps not only aligns your teams, but it also allows you to answer the next two questions (when and where).

Your **velocity** ramps (*people* and *enablement*, as we will discuss shortly) create consistency and predictability for adding new people, ramping them up, and enabling teams to provide a consistent experience for customers, and RevOps gives you the confidence to know when to hire and ramp.

Finally, you're ready to grow and **expand**. This is the final piece of the MOVE framework, taking what you've created and expanding it to new locations and new markets, with new products and services. Your original flying machine has become a fleet of reliable airplanes, and you're ready to take more people to more travel destinations around the world.

In a sense, once you've identified your next best area for growth, you're starting the MOVE framework all over again. It's not a start-and-stop process but a continuous, circular movement for *FLYWHEEL* your company. It's a giant wheel that keeps turning, moving you forward from market to market, and the spokes of that wheel are the four questions: who (market), what (operations), when (velocity), where (expansion).

With these four questions, you'll know everything you need to know to take your next big step.

⟶

4 Question Go-to-market Framework

With these four questions, you'll know everything you need to know to take your next big step.

Let's look at each of the questions in depth so you can begin to discover your own answers.

MARKET:
WHOM SHOULD WE MARKET TO?

To answer this question, we have to return to one of our common misconceptions. As we said earlier, it's not the total target market that drives business outcomes but the *relevancy* of your target market. Think of it this way: It's the difference between firing a hundred arrows in a general direction and hoping a few will hit a target, or taking careful aim at the bull's-eye and ensuring that every arrow hits home. Remember, your arrows are limited to your resources. As you grow and progress through the three Ps, you'll add more arrows to your quiver and more teams of archers, allowing you to go after multiple segments across many categories.

So how do we begin to answer the question of relevancy?

➢ **Relevancy starts with gathering better data about your best customers so you can gain a full picture of them in the best way possible.**

Ideally, this not only tells you if the account is relevant, but it also reveals the best timing for reaching out to them.

To use our airplane metaphor again, if you want to expand your fleet to new destinations, you're not just going to start building airports in random locations around the globe. You can create a beautiful new terminal for your airline on a deserted island in the Arctic Ocean, but almost nobody is going to use it.

Instead, you're going to acquire data from relevant customers (or potential customers) to discover where you should expand in order to better serve them. Now you have your ideal customer, new market, and you've timed your outreach.

That's the essence of how it works in every industry. If you want to enter a new market, you have to identify your ideal customer and then time your outreach. In the B2B world, this will probably be companies that look like companies who have been happy with your products in the past.

Once you determine their relevance, you can use intent data to figure out if now is the right time to go after them.

Intent data tells you all kinds of interesting things about the target account: *CUSTOMERS*

- Are they visiting your website?

- Do they already know your brand?

- Are they looking for a solution like yours?

- If the target account is an existing customer, are they seeing value?

- How well do your teams interact with them?

- Do they respond to your calls?

- Do they have meetings with you?

In other words, you're identifying all of the behavioral signals that the target customer has in their interactions with your company.

We'll look at how you can forage for this kind of intent data. But first, we need a way to categorize all of the accounts in your target market so you can determine which ones need your focus.

To do that, we will use the following terms:

- **Total Addressable Market (TAM):** These are all of the customers you *could* pursue over the next five to ten years. TAM is often used to describe large market opportunities, but it lacks prioritization or actionability.

- **Total Relevant Market (TRM):** These are the customers you *should* pursue now because they're your best-fit target accounts, and they present the highest priority opportunities today. Bear in mind, your TRM will grow in size over time as you win more customers and scale your business.

- ▶ **Intent Accounts:** These are companies that have shown intent toward purchasing your product or product like yours. Think of them as being "in market" to some degree or another. You should be pursuing them with your outbound marketing and sales efforts, even if they're not in your pipeline yet.

- ▶ **In-Pipeline Accounts:** These companies have started taking actions that suggest they are in the market to purchase a product like yours, and your sales team is already interacting with them.

These terms will give you a way to categorize all of the accounts that are out there in your target market.

Your goal is to progress target accounts toward becoming in-pipeline accounts based on their relevancy and readiness.

Prioritizing a market segment

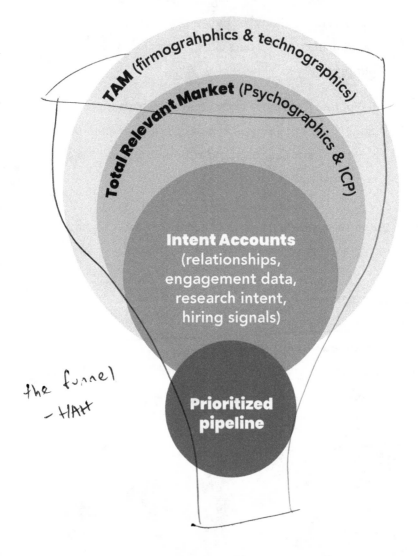

TAM (firmograhphics & technographics)

Total Relevant Market (Psychographics & ICP)

Intent Accounts
(relationships,
engagement data,
research intent,
hiring signals)

**Prioritized
pipeline**

the funnel
— HAH

How are you going to expand your airline company to new travel destinations? As we said, you're not just going to start building airport terminals in as many random locations around the world as possible. Instead, you're going to gather data that reveals some key locations where great new customer opportunities are available.

Among those opportunities, let's say you discover that a bunch of your loyal customers (and potential customers) would greatly appreciate a direct flight from Berlin to Oslo. The data also indicates that this will be the easiest target for you to hit for a variety of reasons.

The answer to *who* seems clear.

Intent data not only tells you which of your target accounts are ready to buy; it also reveals new accounts you'll want to target based on a slew of factors that play into their propensity to buy from you at any given moment. This makes your sales team more efficient, with shorter sales cycles, fewer resources used, and ultimately the ability to provide a more personalized and helpful solution to your new customers.

And now, at last, you have what you need to move a few key intent accounts into your pipeline.

Let's look at some of the specific kinds of data you need to gather.

Total Addressable Market (TAM)

▶ **Firmographic Data:** Look at the target account's number of employees, locations, revenue size, their funding structure, as well as the industry and verticals they play in.

▶ **Technographic Data:** Look at a target account's technology investments, including the types of software and hardware they use, as well as the vendors they currently use, to discover if their current tech is complementary to your solution. Are they coming up for renewal on a competitor's solution? Can you predict if they will add a new solution in the future?

Total Relevant Market (TRM)

TAM data doesn't reveal which customers are relevant today. It only reveals a *possible* future, so now you need TRM data to identify which of those TAM customers are the best fit for your solution.

> *You need TRM data to identify which of those TAM customers are the best fit for your solution.*

▶ **Ideal Customer Profile Attributes:** To determine your TRM, you need to set the criteria for your ideal customer segments, which defines the target customers that your organization is solving for. What qualities make them the best fit for your solution? What data can you utilize to help identify these accounts by name? Understanding your ideal customer profile is key to aligning your revenue team around a segment with coordinated marketing, selling, and servicing.

▸ **Psychographic Data:** This cutting-edge approach utilizes the observed data found in a company's messaging across all publicly available web properties to determine its similarity with your existing customers or account segments. It reveals the interests and intentions of a target company based on the keyword-trending natural language processing (NLP) in their messages in the market, helping you find the most relevant accounts within your TAM—even identifying great accounts that traditional firmographics segmentation would fail to find.

Intent Accounts

Once you've figured out your TRM, you will probably still be dealing with a lot of companies you could potentially pursue. You need to narrow the focus even further so you know whom to market to *next*.

Use intent data to narrow the focus even further.

- **Engagement:** What first-party interactions is the target account having with your brand? In particular, look at the interaction rate between your brand and the target account so you can prioritize the one showing the most engagement.

- **Hiring:** Is the target account hiring or posting jobs? Are there open positions in the company relevant to the benefits of your solution? This will reveal what they are focused on and investing in so you can predict if they are in market and adjust your messaging accordingly.

- **Research:** What content consumption habits or trends do you see with the target company? What content are employees consuming or showing interest in? This can reveal which accounts show intent but might not yet be aware of your brand.

- **Relationship:** Is the target account interacting with your employees? How many two-way interactions have they had with your brand? Look at the frequency, recency, and velocity of these interactions so you can determine which ones have the strongest potential relationship.

With TRM, you have a better way to prioritize the best accounts than your otherwise unwieldy TAM, accounts that are a better fit because they look and act like customers you've recently won. However, even TRM might give you more accounts than your limited resources can focus on. That's where intent comes in, identifying the accounts within your TRM that are already in the market to buy.

And that's how you answer the first question of the MOVE framework: Whom should we market to?

Bear in mind, if you're in the *ideation* stage of your business, you will primarily focus on TAM, but as you move into the *transition* stage, you need to shift your focus to TRM and then to specific segments within your TRM.

Got it?

Okay, Berlin to Oslo, here we come!

OPERATIONS: WHAT DO WE NEED TO OPERATE EFFECTIVELY?

When we speak of "operations" we're really talking specifically about RevOps. Keep that in mind. Remember, the goal of GTM is to create high-performing revenue teams.

What is the goal of RevOps? To discern the truth of the numbers over and above the mere opinions of people so the business can make accurate decisions.

In a sense, this is the brain of the MOVE framework, and it consists of **repeatable processes**, **data**, your **systems** and **tech stack**, and a set of **metrics** that allows you to determine where things are going.

So what do you need to operate effectively? That's the question that must be answered at this point in order to take your next step as an organization.

Let's take a look at how you can begin to answer this question. To begin, we'll address a couple of wrong approaches to operations that are all too common.

First, companies tend to think of operations as an efficiency metric, but we recommend leveling up your thinking and approaching operations not for *efficiency* but for *effectiveness*. There's a big difference between operating your business efficiently and operating your business effectively, as we will see.

Approach operations not for efficiency but for effectiveness.

Second, companies often have *marketing* operations and *sales* operations sitting in their own individual departments because they think it'll make things more efficient. It seems to make sense, doesn't it? Let each team do whatever they have to do in order to operate quickly.

Marketing operations needs to focus on things like creating great landing pages, connecting them to the customer relationship management (CRM) platform, and making the data flow properly, while sales ops needs to focus on things like data hygiene and sales analytics.

Enter RevOps!

Revenue Operations:
The New Leader of Go-to-Market

Now, we love running polls, and we were curious what groups leaders think belong in RevOps. The results were encouraging:

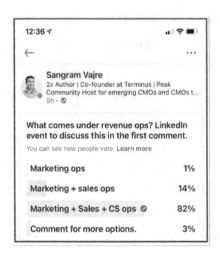

Yes, in the brave new world of GTM, sales, marketing, *and* customer success function as a unified, high-performing revenue team with a silo-free focus on RevOps. Rather than trying to do everything as efficiently as possible for their individual departments, they work together to create an *effective* business model for the entire company.

To do that, they must work together well so they can discern where the company should be heading, in what they should be investing, what's working and not working, what systems are duplicates, and so on.

The question is, how can you take the information you've learned about customers from marketing and sales and put it in the hands of customer success so they can figure out what's working and what isn't? How do you get the data from customer success issues about bad customers back to marketing and sales? This two-way exchange of data is very hard when your teams are siloed.

In fact, this difficulty might be the exact reason why you feel stuck at a certain stage of your business maturity. It's also the reason why sales and marketing are providing different numbers and contradictory data, then spending an inordinate amount of time trying to justify them, rather than working from a single source of truth.

"We've got the right data," Marketing says. "Our data is current."

"No, our data says something different," Sales replied, "and it's more current than yours."

If you don't have a single source of truth by the time you get to the transition stage of GTM maturity, if the silos are still firmly in place, you're *done for*.

Can we put it any more bluntly than that? This is where people get stuck, sometimes permanently. This is where the airplanes stall out and drop from the sky, or to put it more broadly, this is when your new airport terminal becomes a ghost town because customers aren't flying there.

Therefore, we propose that in the new world, you knock the silos down and bring these teams together. Create that new role—RevOps—to lead this operations team and have them report to either the CFO or COO—possibly even the CEO—rather than any of the team leaders, so that this new revenue leader can act independently without any bias toward a specific function. Otherwise, they will tend to focus on their own department rather than overall business outcomes.

According to TOPO, "Revenue Operations is the modern operating model for driving efficient, predictable revenue by using an interconnected, observable, end-to-end process."[2]

> *Revenue Operations is the*
> *modern operating model for driving*
> *efficient, predictable revenue by using*
> *an interconnected, observable,*
> *end-to-end process.*

Here's what that new org structure might look like:

---

[2] Craig Rosenberg and Dan Gottlieb, "Revenue Operations Framework: The Critical Elements of a World-Class Revenue Operations Organization," TOPO, August 31, 2020.

REV-OPS
Sample Org

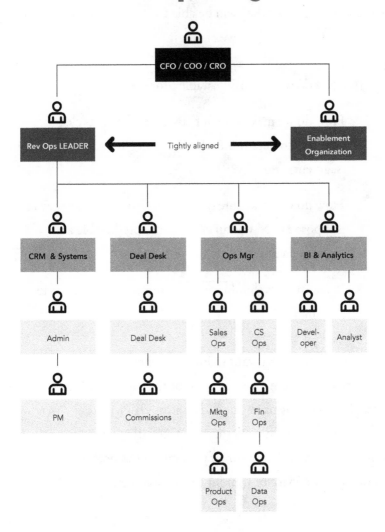

Although the revenue leader provides support for marketing, sales, and customer success, they need to operate independently, without bias toward any specific department, so they can focus on the overall effectiveness of the business model. That objectivity and alignment are how they will be able to answer questions like the following:

- How do we create repeatable processes?

- How do we make sure our customer data is as clean as possible to determine what's working for which segments and why?

- How do we make sure our systems work the way they're supposed to so we can create more predictable and reliable data?

- What metrics should we use to measure our success in the market?

Of course, you don't want to lose efficiency. Indeed, the focus on effectiveness doesn't have to come at the expense of being able to crank out landing pages, move data around quickly, build weighted forecasts, or launch NPS surveys. You still need a representative ops leader for each division of your revenue team, but it's all being done in the service of your business outcomes.

When done well, your new aligned revenue team—marketing, sales, and customer success—gains a perspective on the overall performance of the business, as well as the performance of individual teams, so they can make decisions about where to invest next. In doing so, you get to one source of truth.

Imagine if you didn't have every department bringing their own numbers into the boardroom so you then had to piece them together somehow to create an overall picture of the business. What if, instead, you had a single leader, RevOps, who presented you with a scorecard that revealed the health of the overall business at a glance.

Bear in mind, if you're in the *ideation* stage of business maturity, you might be just fine with *only* marketing ops and sales ops. After all, you're just getting off the launch ramp. However, once you move into the *transition* stage, it becomes absolutely imperative that you bring sales, marketing, and customer success together as soon as possible. The success of your business will demand it. Therefore, you should have RevOps in mind even in the *ideation* stage.

So how do you answer the question, "What do we need to operate effectively?"

The answer is simple:

Create RevOps to support marketing, sales, and customer success, and put the right elements into place (*repeatable processes, data*, your *systems* and *tech stack*, and a set of *metrics* that allows you to determine where things are going), and you'll have what you need to operate your next move as an organization.

Here are what those elements might look like depending on where you're at along the GTM maturity curve:

Ideation (Problem-Market Fit)

▸ **Metrics by functions:** Sales activities (calls, demos, opportunities), marketing activities (traffic and leads), funnel conversion rates and cost-per-lead, bookings and win rate.

▸ **Tech:** Customer relationship management (CRM), marketing automation (MAP) conversation tracking, content management system (CMS), sales automation, and contact data.

Here's a sample scorecard for the *ideation* stage:

Sales-led
SCORECARD

Branding	Inbound Funnel	Conversion Metrics	Outbound Funnel	Revenue KPI's

Inbound Calls & Emails

35
Month

Qualified Conversions

350 vs. 400
Month

Site Conversion Rate

5.70%
Quarter

Outbound Engagement Rate

3%
Month

Revenue vs. Goal

1.3M vs. 1.5M
Month

Site Traffic

6,090
Month

Top Inbound Campaigns

Partner Webinar: 50
Demo Request: 45
Customer Referral: 40
Month

Lead to Qual.
Conversion Rate

50%
Month

Average Deal Size

$55,000
Quarter

Engagement Spikes

300 Accounts
Month

Outbound Opportunities

65 vs. 85
Month

Opportunity Close Rate

25%
Quarter

Transition (Product-Market Fit)

▸ **Metrics by account segments:** Ideation metrics + engagement, pipeline coverage, deal velocity, average deal size, gross retention rate (GRR), efficiency metrics (magic number, customer acquisition cost), calculated per segment.

▸ **Tech:** Ideation tech + ABM platform, intent data, intelligence data, multichannel delivery, business analytics, sales enablement and automated training (learning management system and coaching), "configure, price, quote," order management, billing automation, and customer service automation.

Here's a sample scorecard for the *transition* stage:

EXECUTIVE CMO–CRO SCORECARD

Branding	Inbound Funnel	Conversion Metrics	Outbound Funnel	Revenue KPI's
Inbound Calls & Emails 35 Month	**Qualified Conversions** 350 vs. 400 Month	**Site Conversion Rate** 5.70% Quarter	**Outbound Engagement Rate** 3% Month	**Revenue vs. Goal** 1.3M vs. 1.5M Month
Site Traffic 6,090 Month	**Top Inbound Campaigns** Partner Webinar: 50 Demo Request: 45 Customer Referral: 40 Month	**Lead to Qual. Conversion Rate** 50% Month	**Engaged Target Accounts** 1,225 out of 3,500 Month	**Average Deal Size** $55,000 Quarter
Engagement Spikes 300 Accounts Month	**Inbound Opportunities** 45 vs. 60 Month	**Target Acct. Engagement Rate** 25% Quarter	**Outbound Opportunities** 65 vs. 85 Month	**Opportunity Close Rate** 25% Quarter
Share of Voice 33% Quarter	**Inbound Pipeline Gen.** $1,687,500 Month	**Deals advancing to Discovery** 75 vs. 95 Month	**Outbound Pipeline** $2,275,000 Month	**Pipeline Velocity** 72 days Quarter
Net Promoter Score 7.5 Quarter	**Inbound Pipeline Coverage** 2.5x Open Pipeline = x	**Deals advancing to Proposal** 40 vs. 50 Month	**Outbound Pipeline Coverage** 2x Open Pipeline = x	**Cost per Opportunity** $250 Quarter

Execution
(Platform-Market Fit)

- **Metrics by customer cohorts:** Transition metrics + customer lifetime value (CLV), time to value, net promote score (NPS), customer ROI, product line revenue and pipeline, net revenue retention (NRR)/net expansion, gross margins, growth by category.

- **Tech:** Execution tech + customer data platform (CDP), integrated stack, data stack with AI/ML modeling, customer experience management, full journey orchestration, sales forecasting.

Here's a sample scorecard for the *execution* stage:

GTM EXEC SCORECARD

Net Retention	Total Net Growth ARR	New ARR	Expansion ARR	Product Usage
Net Retention Leader Forecast **90%** forecasting 90% of goal	Total New ARR Leader Forecast **10M** forecasting 100% of goal	New ARR Leader Forecast **7M** forecasting 100% of goal	Expansion ARR Leader Forecast **3M** forecasting 100% of goal	Product Usage Forecast **10,000** Monthly Active Users
Gross Retention ARR Closed Won **$4,350,000**	Closed Won Total ARR **$2,500,000**	Closed Won New Business ARR **$2,000,000**	Closed Won Expansion ARR **$500,000**	Monthly Active Users **9,500**
Customer Success QLs **67**	Total Open Pipeline **35M**	Total Open New Pipe **25M**	Total Open Expn Pipeline **10M**	Product Qualified QLs **50**
Weighted Pipeline GRR **69%**	Product line A/B/C Status **47% vs. goal 60%**	Leading New ARR Product Line **80% to goal**	Leading Expansion Product Line **70% to goal**	Customers — Usage Red Flag **13**
Overall Weighted Pipeline **$10,030,005**	ARR by Segment **45% Enterprise 55% SMB**	New Pipeline Funnel Efficiency **Average Age: 90 days**	Expansion Funnel Efficiency **Average Age: 40 days**	Gross Margin Current Qtr. **75%**
Customer Acct. Engagement **75% engagement**	A Account Engagement **88% engagement**	B Account Engagement **45% engagement**	Top 100 Accounts Campaign **76% engagement**	Prospect Intent Trends **350 intent accounts**

Those elements are what you need to operate effectively no matter what your industry or niche, even if you're trying to build a fleet of commercial airlines to take passengers all over the world.

Operations metrics and tech by stage

Ideation	Transition	Execution
(problem-market)	(product-market)	(platform-market)

Metrics by functions

Sales activities
(calls, demo's, ops)
Marketing activities
(traffic, leads)
Funnel Conv rates
& cost per lead
Bookings & Win rate

Metrics by Segments

Engagement
Pipeline coverage
Deal velocity
Average deal size
GRR
Efficiency metrics
(magic number, CAC)

Metrics by customer cohorts

CLV, Time to value,
NPS, Customer ROI
Product line revenue
& Pipeline
NRR / Net Expansion
Gross Margins
Growth by category

Tech: CRM, conversation tracking, CMS & MA, Sales automation, contact data

Tech: Ideation Tech + ABM, intent data, intelligence data, Multi channel, Bi Analytics, Sales enablement & automated training - LMS / Coaching, CPQ/order mgmt , billing automation, CS automation)
(non integrated / iframed)

Tech: Transition Tech + CDP, integrated stack, AI/ML data stack, Customer Experience Management, Sales Forecasting

VELOCITY: WHEN CAN WE SCALE OUR BUSINESS?

It's a question that haunts almost every business leader: "When can we scale our business/structure/system/people?" We interviewed hundreds of business leaders across key stakeholder positions and found that some variation of this question is on the mind of almost every business leader almost all the time.

This question is on the mind
of almost every business leader
almost all the time.

Velocity helps you answer this question. Actually, it answers almost all of your "when" questions.

As the old saying goes, "Time kills all great ideas." In every interview we conducted, leaders across a wide array of companies felt /feared the impending nature of this quote. Why are they so tormented by velocity questions? Because of the constant concern that there is some amazing growth opportunity right in front of them that they're not seeing or not moving on fast enough. The door is open, but it's an automatic swinging door. If they don't spot the door and go through it fast enough, it'll swing shut and lock, and the opportunity will be lost.

Yes, time kills all great ideas, so if you don't know when to make your next move, you might miss the opportunity. This is the essence of velocity.

On the flip side, if you enter a door too early, it might not be open wide enough yet, and you'll smash right into it. In practical terms, that usually means burning through cash, losing focus, or wrecking your metrics. You have to know when the door is open enough for you to go through.

And that is *also* the essence of velocity.

To complicate matters, there are two velocity ramps that you have to create: the people ramp and the enablement ramp. Let's look at each of them.

> There are two velocity ramps that you have to create: the people ramp and the enablement ramp.

People Ramp

Your people ramp determines how fast your people get things done and achieve success in their individual roles. It answers questions like these:

- When you hire a new team member, how quickly can you get them to own a project?

- When you add someone to your customer success team, how quickly can you get them to upsell, up-serve, or expand the deal to level up existing accounts and make them bigger?

- When you hire a new salesperson, how quickly can you ramp up their quota and exceed it?

- When you hire a new marketing team member, how quickly can you get them to generate demand and drive awareness of the business?

The people ramp also tells you how quickly you can get customers to see the value of a product, because after all, you want your customers to see ROI as quickly as possible.

But your people ramp deals with only half the problem. You also need an enablement ramp for your high-performing revenue team.

Enablement Ramp

Your enablement ramp is about figuring out what to do with your marketing, sales, and customer success teams, including training, documentation, decks, playbooks, kickoffs, and quarterly business reviews. In other words, how do you enable your high-performing revenue team to be successful?

equip
inner
success

If you don't get this right, you won't be able to scale, which means you'll burn people out and create poor customer experiences.

The real questions of enablement are, "How quickly can we enable marketing, sales, and customer success, and how effective is our process for doing so?"

Too often, companies ask the wrong questions first. They want to scale, so they ask, "How many salespeople do we need to hire?" That's getting the cart before the horse. Or more appropriately, it's like getting the propeller on your flying machine to spin before you attach the wings. What you should ask first is, "How quickly can we get our salespeople to reach their quota?"

Instead of just adding new people in order to scale, first figure out how quickly your existing people can scale. Then you will know how many people to hire.

Why? Because you can't just hire marketing, sales, and customer success people and expect them to work with each other at a high performance level. Inevitably, it's going to break down into finger-pointing and blame.

You can't just hire marketing, sales, and customer success people and expect them to work with each other at a high performance level.

Marketing will say things like, "The product is ready to launch. Sales needs to get on the ball and start pitching this thing!"

And Sales will reply, "We don't have the latest pricing and messaging from the marketing team, so how can we start pitching the new product?"

And Customer Success will say, "We're not ready to onboard new customers because our team hasn't been trained yet and doesn't know how to communicate the value!"

This kind of back-and-forth blame happens constantly in companies that lack a proper enablement process. Each function is running independently at their own speed.

You've probably seen the pit crews that work at NASCAR races. A pit crew is comprised of smaller teams and individuals each with their own specific focus. You've got the jackman, the front and rear tire changers, the gas man, and quite a few others behind the wall. Typically, pit crew members work very well together, so when a race car pulls into the pit, they can refuel, change the tires, check for other problems, and get the car back out onto the track in a matter of seconds.

Can you imagine how it would go if each team in the pit crew operated at their own speed with widely varying skill levels? Everyone would be tripping over each other, pointing fingers, struggling to coordinate, and the whole thing would move a lot slower. It might even end in catastrophe.

The same is true of every commercial airplane. Before a plane takes off, the flight crew and ground staff go through an elaborate process of making sure it's in good shape and ready to go. Individuals and small teams go to work loading baggage and cargo, servicing the cabin, running engineering checks, checking safety equipment, testing all of the flight instruments. This procedure requires the right tools and training, coordination, and a lot of cooperation, because if anyone fails to do their job well, it could put the well-being of passengers and crew in danger.

For an individual passenger to take that new flight from Berlin to Oslo, a whole bunch of people on multiple teams have to work together to make it possible. An enablement ramp makes sure that every member of the crew is up to speed, thoroughly trained and ready to do their job at a high performance level so the airplane can fly safely, reliably, and on time.

 As we said in the beginning, GTM is the vehicle for delivering your company's mission and vision to customers, and your people become your brand ambassadors. Most of your customers' experience with your brand will come through your people, like it or not. So when you don't ramp effectively, when you don't enable effectively, then you're either going to miss opportunities because you lack the people to take advantage of them or you will deliver a subpar experience because your people aren't trained properly.

GTM is the vehicle for delivering your company's mission and vision to customers, and your people become your brand ambassadors.

This is why velocity matters. This is why you need to get your ramps right.

To use another sports metaphor, think about an Olympic rowing team. You want everyone to be thoroughly trained and rowing in unison in the same direction. Even if most of the team is doing a great job, if one or two people are rowing in the wrong direction or rowing out of sync with everyone else, then the forward momentum of the entire boat will be hindered.

When your ramp is right, every person across your marketing, sales, and customer success teams will use the same messaging, even the same words, at every touchpoint with customers.

what are our "same words"?

The same words show up on the website as in the sales deck. The same words show up during implementation and when a customer success team member talks to a customer. None of this happens without an enablement organization, and as with RevOps, it should be centralized outside of marketing, sales, and success by the time you reach the execution stage.

When you get this kind of consistency across all of your teams, then you have velocity. Everyone is rowing in sync, in the same direction, and the boat cuts smoothly through the water at maximum speed toward the finish line.

"There's a Fire, So You're Hired"

Too often, companies run by the motto, "There's a fire, so you're hired." When there's a problem in one of their teams, they hire to "fix" the problem. That's like the rowing team just adding more rowers to make up for one team member who is rowing in the wrong direction.

"Well, if we shove ten more rowers into the boat, they'll compensate for the one or two who are trying to make us go backward." Without realizing it, this is the kind of logic being employed.

It's not just ineffective; it's also a negative approach to growing your teams because it's reactive. However, it's the way most companies operate. Identify which team has the biggest fire, then hire another person for that team. If the product team is on fire, then the product team gets to hire another engineer. If the sales team is on fire, add another salesperson.

This reactive model is constantly trying to fix what's already broken instead of hiring ahead of the next great opportunity. So how about a better approach? How about getting the velocity right so you're hiring ahead of new customers and enabling your people to meet the market at just the right time?

To do that, you need proven processes, with a model and data that has been analyzed by your RevOps team, and the ability for your teams to move, hire, and perform. That way, you have the confidence that when you hire more people, you're doing it because of the company strategy based on the execution of insights from operations. That's the key to getting your velocity right, and when you're at velocity, you'll feel confident about making investments in people because you know you'll hit the targets those people are lined up for.

Let's suppose you're planning a new product launch. Here are the kinds of questions you need to be asking in order to enable your revenue team:

> What will the sales team *not* do (or do less of) to make room for this new launch? (Teams can only consume so much. Prioritize and make tradeoffs for the key focus areas of your GTM team. What is enabled must be part

of the strategy, and the company needs to be focused and selective about what the team will take to market.)

▶ How much airtime do we need to schedule to keep it top of mind for GTM teams?

▶ Which gaps must enablement overcome in order to enact the strategy?

  → Knowledge

  → Throughput

  → Product

  → Market

▶ What is the level of difficulty for enablement (i.e., how much is new)?

  → New products

  → New competitors

  → New value statement

  → New personas

  → New market segment

▶ How will you resource the launch? Existing teams, additional resources, or overlay teams?

▶ How will you measure the launch (the enactment of our strategy)?

One thing to keep in mind is that the focus of your enablement ramps will change depending on where you are in the GTM maturity curve.

In the IDEATION STAGE, you focus on "putting out fires." You can't predict them yet.

In the TRANSITION STAGE, you focus on improving your selling and services.

In the EXECUTION STAGE, you focus on improving the customer experience.

As we mentioned earlier, in B2B, customers typically go through a series of handoffs on their path to purchase, success, and lifetime value, but without proper ramps in place, the overarching customer experience lacks consistency. We believe the future of B2B will involve fewer handoffs, and when they occur, customers won't feel like they're starting all over again because GTM will create a greater sense of consistency across marketing, sales, and customer success.

When you get this right, there comes a point where all of your gears are working together from the start of conversion and throughout the customer journey. You can now forecast better, so you're getting predictable business where you can line up your conversions toward expansion.

You're right where the finance team predicted you would be at the end of the last quarter, and you're able to duplicate this for multiple quarters in a row. There's a method to the madness because you have consistent processes in place, and since you're able to forecast the upcoming quarters, you can begin thinking about expansion. Once you've reached this point, it's time to figure out where you can grow the most next.

There's a natural flow in the MOVE framework that leads to this point:

1) First, you figure out your market.

2) Then you get your operations in place.

3) Now you have confidence to move at velocity.

Let's suppose your first plan was to sell into the mid-market in North America. You came up with a plan and processes, and now you're starting to achieve it. You're experiencing success in the market consistently, so now you're ready to grow and expand into new markets, new products, new services, and new verticals (or, shall we say, new airport terminals, new and improved airplanes, and improved services for passengers).

Velocity opens up expansion.

Your people and enablement ramps are in place, delivering consistent ROI from a consistent customer experience at every touchpoint. Everything is done in the service of strategy, and all of the silos have been torn down. You have the ability to forecast, so you now know *when* to make your next move.

You're ready for the next and final stage of the MOVE framework: *expansion*.

EXPANSION: WHERE CAN WE GROW THE MOST?

So now it's time to determine your next move, and expansion is about figuring out where your next best opportunity lies. No company wants to stop growing. We've never met a business executive who said, "Well, we don't want to expand anymore. We're not interested in new markets or new products. We're satisfied being completely static. We like going nowhere."

> *Expansion is about figuring out where your next best opportunity lies.*

Of course, many businesses *are* static. They're going nowhere fast, but it's not because they want it. They didn't plan on being static. They simply don't know how to expand.

What we typically hear from frustrated leaders is, "We really want to expand, but we don't know how." They don't know which opportunity to pursue next, which one will provide the most growth, or they're struggling to handle the growth. Worst of all, maybe they've tried to expand, but they didn't answer the MOVE questions, so the expansion failed. They launched the wrong product, or entered the wrong market, or launched too early (or too late).

Whatever the case, the expansion became a massive distraction and created downward momentum, and now they're wary of making similar mistakes. This is a source of tension for many companies.

Chances are, you've had some expansion frustrations in your own company. It's a common problem—a new market, vertical, product, or service that just doesn't work out. Perhaps these disappointments made you timid or anxious about further expansion, but it'll be different the next time you try it. Why? Because now you have the MOVE framework and you know which questions to answer in order to expand *the right way*.

So let's begin by laying all of the cards on the table.

There are essentially three ways you can expand:

- Expansion with sales
- Expansion with coverage
- Expansion with solutions

Let's look at each of these so you can figure out your next best opportunity.

The first way you can grow is through **sales**, and indeed, this is an extremely popular approach to business growth. There have been countless books written on the subject. Chances are, you've read a few of them. We've written on the topic ourselves quite a bit.

Typically, the growth model looks something like this.

You start with direct sales, then add referral partners, then build out channel partner and agency programs, and all along you're incrementally building capacity outside the walls of your company (if you're doing a great job as a business). In the process, your partners, network, and other external distribution vehicles create nonlinear growth, which means you don't just have to keep adding more salespeople in order to get the next twenty customers.

Essentially, this approach recognizes that you can hire only so many salespeople to scale, so you have to find a way to make your sales as widely distributed as possible. This has been a very successful model for many companies. HubSpot, for example, as reported in 2017, had 40 percent of their revenue from their partner program.[3] Similarly, more than 50 percent of sales for the data warehousing company Snowflake are "partner-assisted."[4]

> *You have to find a way to make your sales*
> *as widely distributed as possible.*

The second way you can grow is to increase **coverage**. A company that has had success in North America might decide to take their products and services to an Asian market, for example. Or they might expand into a different vertical. Maybe they've had success in the manufacturing industry, but now they decide to take their products or services to the financial industry.

They might also move upmarket (reaching customers with larger needs and budgets) or downmarket (reaching customers with less complex needs and leaner budgets). In B2B, going upmarket generally means moving from small businesses to mid-market

---

[3] Peter Caputa, "How I Built a $100M+ Sales Channel by Challenging the Status Quo," Think Growth, January 2, 2017, https://thinkgrowth.org/how-i-built-a-100m-sales-channel-by-challenging-the-status-quo-e82000e9179d.

[4] Rick Whiting, "Snowflake Launches First Partner Program, Creates Resell and MSP Opportunities," CRN, June 16, 2020, https://www.crn.com/news/channel-programs/snowflake-launches-first-partner-program-creates-resell-and-msp-opportunities.

companies to enterprises. Sometimes you might have an enterprise-class product, but you go downmarket in order to generate product-led growth (think Slack, Calendly, and Dropbox).

For example, during the pandemic, Zoom became a household name overnight by going downmarket as they opened up their product to schools, students, and regular folks. The product was originally intended for small and mid-market B2B companies, and that's where the value of Zoom first came from. As they got product fit, they began advertising in airports and other places where they might reach executives, and they added features like enterprise-level security as they moved up into the enterprise segment.

Then COVID-19 rocked the world, and Zoom's simple and elegant solution began attracting B2C, nonprofits, and governments. Seeing the sudden (and massive) need for their product, the company expanded into these new segments, became the de facto form of communication for socially distanced everything, and had tremendous success. Now they are launching new products like Zoom Phone for businesses and adding webinar capabilities as they seek to build out a much broader platform.

Salesforce, on the other hand, went upmarket throughout their history. They started out offering their classic CRM platform to small businesses, but gradually they moved their focus upmarket as they reached out with the enterprise version of their platform. Finally, they expanded into B2C and spread around the globe.

Is it time for you to expand your coverage? At this point, you should be measuring what percentage of your revenue is coming from each coverage area. How can you increase your annual contract value (ACV)? How do you sell multiyear deals? How do you get prepaid commitments? All of these will allow you to increase the value of your business so you can go to a bigger market and create bigger valuation.

> *At this point, you should be measuring*
> *what percentage of your revenue is*
> *coming from each coverage area.*

The third way you can grow is through increased **solutions**. This is also very common. Indeed, almost every successful company grows from a single-product point solution to a multiple-product platform solution. There's only so much mileage you can get out of your existing product because you're trying to sell the same thing to the same customers. Also, as competition or consolidation grows in the market, you face more challenges to differentiate yourself.

How, then, do you know when and where to create new solutions, which new categories to move into, and when to acquire new companies? You will make smarter expansion decisions when you understand your center of gravity better than the adjacent category players around you. Indeed, if you can figure out what will naturally consolidate around *your* platform rather than *other* category platforms, you will make decisions that create value instead of confusion.

> *You will make smarter expansion*
> *decisions when you understand your center*
> *of gravity better than the adjacent*
> *category players around you.*

For category expansion moves, ask yourself the following questions and map out your potential moves (and the potential moves of both current and future competitors).

Category Expansion—
Key Questions before You Build,
Buy, or Partner

Category Depth: What will make your existing customers happier (i.e., deliver on your promises)?

Adjacent Niche: What additional use cases could you solve that expand your platform value?

Emerging Categories: Which emerging categories and vendors could you partner with to grow faster with an eye toward future mergers and acquisitions (M&A)? Where are consolidations likely to occur?

Established Categories: Which established categories and vendors are likely to enter your space and how should you prepare both opportunistically and defensively? Who has center of gravity?

Category Expansion

Your Category	Adjacent Niche	Emerging Categories	Established Categories

Category depth

Category strategy is one thing, but really understanding what you are acquiring is something else altogether. Although M&A can be exciting and hugely beneficial, it can also be costly, poorly executed, or massively distracting. The following guide will help you assess your target acquisitions and remind you what you are solving for (and what to watch out for).

Considering the role of M&A to expand and grow

Acquiring for?	What are you getting?	Why do it?	What to watch out for?
Product	• Tuck-in or product line • Depth or breadth • New personas or use cases • Platform assets	Product Strategy	• mis aligned with ICP • high feature overlap • comes with tech debt • disjointed user experience
Customers	• Market share • Expand market (up,down,over)	Revenue / Marquee Brands	• risks on existing revenue • difficulty of migration or cross sell • bad fit customers
Teams	• Key talent / leaders • Domain expertise • Departmental strength • Location coverage	Energy / Gaps / Scale	• not a culture fit • irreversible fatigue • won't buy in to your mission
Platform	• New category and market • Product(s), customers, & teams • Enterprise value	Big Expansion	• org complexity & incompatibility • forced reaction from competitors • employee or market disillusionment

Remember, the more expansive the distribution strategy, the bigger the opportunity. Also, you may be able to take your existing solution and package it up in a better way to reach more customers, as Zoom did when they responded to the needs of schools.

Look at the growth opportunities before you, whether through increased sales, coverage, or adding new solutions, and determine which of them offers the next best area of growth potential.

Whether you decide to grow through sales, coverage, or solutions, you have to establish an iterative process that will feed back into your existing teams. Again, it's circular in nature, a wheel that keeps turning along the MOVE framework, because once you expand, you start over at the beginning of the MOVE framework asking the same four questions in order to continue growing.

It's iterative because, along the way, you gain insights from your GTM process that feed back into your company strategy and GTM process, so as the wheel of the MOVE framework continues to turn, your company is ideally getting better and better at it. Remember that new Berlin to Oslo flight you built for your airline? Well, you gained insights from that experience that will feed into your GTM process when you open a new terminal for an Oslo to Madrid flight next year. That's how the wheel (or in this case, the landing gear) keeps turning.

MOVE Framework

1. Market (who) Who should we market to?	**TAM** Broad - minimal prioritization	**Segments** Relevant accounts (TRM + ICP + Intent)	**Cohorts** Customer cohorts + Relevant new accounts
2. Operations (what) What do you need to operate effectively?	**Ad-hoc** Department level data and decision making authority	**Aligned** Shared understanding of the data and aligned decision making across sales & marketing with dedicated ops for each department	**RevOps** Coordinated decision making a cross GTM teams aligned to achieve company objectives led by centralized rev ops team using shared systems, data, processes and GTM scorecard
3. Velocity (when) When can we scale our business?	**Reactive** When there's a fire, hire someone to put it out	**Proactive** Invest now to prevent future fires	**Prioritized** Invest for growth not for pain
4. Expansion (where) Where can we grow the most?	**Single threaded expansion** One distribution path (direct, channel or partner)	**Partial expansion** Multiple distribution paths and coverage areas (GEO's, Verticals)	**Full expansion** Distribution + Coverage + Multiple products, platform, & ecosystem

For GTM to continue serving your company throughout your growth and development, it is imperative that you continue to make these iterative improvements so you're always aiming at the right target in the right way.

Putting it all together:

1) Identify your current business stage.

2) Align to your current GTM focus.

3) Answer the four-question framework to establish your GTM process.

4) Run your business off the KPIs.

5) Last, test your business outcomes. If there's no growth, identify if it is a three Ps problem or a GTM process problem, and invest accordingly. Use the bulleted list under the heading "From Ideation to Transition" in Section Two for things that might be preventing you from transitioning to the next stage. Once you're ready for the next stage, transform your GTM process by repeating these steps again.

Business Stage & the 3Ps

GTM Focus & the team	Ideation Problem-market fit	Transition Product-market fit	Execution Platform-market fit
	Leads Sales-led	**Accounts** Sales & Marketing	**Customers** Customer Success + Sales & Marketing
MOVE Framework **1. Market (who)** Who should we market to?	**TAM** Broad - minimal prioritization	**Segments** Relevant accounts (TRM + ICP + Intent)	**Cohorts** Customer cohorts + Relevant new accounts
2. Operations (what) What do you need to operate effectively?	**Ad-hoc** Department level data and decision making authority	**Aligned** Shared understanding of the data and aligned decision making across sales & marketing with dedicated ops for each department	**RevOps** Coordinated decision making a cross GTM teams aligned to achieve company objectives led by centralized rev ops team using shared systems, data, processes and GTM scorecard
3. Velocity (when) When can we scale our business?	**Reactive** When there's a fire, hire someone to put it out	**Proactive** Invest now to prevent future fires	**Prioritized** Invest for growth not for pain
4. Expansion (where) Where can we grow the most?	**Single threaded expansion** One distribution path (direct, channel or partner)	**Partial expansion** Multiple distribution paths and coverage areas (GEO's, Verticals)	**Full expansion** Distribution + Coverage + Multiple products, platform, & ecosystem
KPI's	**Metrics by functions** Funnel Conv rates, CPL Bookings & Win rate Sales activities (calls, demo's, ops) Marketing activities (traffic, leads)	**Metrics by account segments** Engagement Pipeline coverage Deal velocity Average deal size, GRR Efficiency metrics (magic number, CAC)	**Metrics by customer cohorts** CLV, Time to value, NPS, Customer ROI Product line revenue & Pipeline NRR / Net Expansion Gross Margins Growth by category
Business Outcomes	Inefficient growth	Efficient growth	Efficient growth at scale

Check out themovebook.com to download
assessment, templates, and workbooks
that will help you turn your GTM silos into
a high-performing revenue team.

Section Four

ORCHESTRATING YOUR NEXT MOVE

Align Your Key Stakeholders

WE'VE GIVEN YOU ALL OF THE INDIVIDUAL PIECES OF the MOVE framework. We've even lined them up for you in the right order. We've revealed how the MOVE framework is iterative by design and how it helps you orchestrate your next move as a company, regardless of your stage, size, or complexity.

In order to do this, however, you're going to have to align all of the key stakeholders in your company so everyone is on the same page, with the same perspective about the role of GTM.

Easier said than done, right?

When we began conducting research for this book, interviewing hundreds of business leaders across a wide array of industries, we quickly learned that key stakeholders are not aligned in their thinking about GTM. In fact, their understanding of GTM tends to be influenced by the way they view success.

In this chapter, we're going to speak to your key stakeholders and provide some clear instructions that will help all of your major players get aligned around your GTM process.

Indeed, you may be shocked to discover just how much misalignment exists among the everyday GTM beliefs of most organizational leaders. There's an inherent complexity in the ownership of your GTM process, as well as the role each stakeholder must play.

> *You may be shocked to discover*
> *just how much misalignment exists among*
> *the everyday GTM beliefs of most*
> *organizational leaders.*

Never fear! We're going to clear up the confusion and provide some prescriptive advice for each stakeholder so they know exactly what role they need to play as you transform your GTM team. We'll reveal both (1) what each role needs to do and (2) what to watch out for.

INVESTORS: THE GUIDE

How do investors understand GTM? Ryan Ziegler of Edison Partners, a growth equity firm, defined GTM in this way: "GTM is a process that connects the factory floor to the front office." We quite like that perspective on GTM. However, if you're an investor reading this book, we want to be very clear about one thing: your job is to make sure you're *not* trying to own the GTM process. Your job is to help the CEO by empowering *them* to own it.

> *GTM is a process that*
> *connects the factory floor to*
> *the front office.*

Kelly Ford from Edison Partners explained the role of investors in the GTM process in this way: "As former go-to-marketers, we play the role of guide, and we have a bird's-eye view into what some companies are doing right and what other companies are doing wrong." Edison offers their portfolio companies access to a center of excellence to help them implement and optimize GTM.

Kelly shared with us the framework for Edison's GTM center of excellence.

GO TO MARKET
Center of Excellence

STRATEGY > **POSITION** > **PLAN** > **OPERATIONS**

Size and segmentation of market, account, and buyer characteristics, business and GTM model, and aligned unit economics.

How solutions fit in the market, including buyer problems being addressed and competitive differentiation.

Growth levers, revenue and cost assumptions, and initiatives for strategic alignment.

Consistent processes, motions, measurement operationalized for volume, value, velocity.

ORG DESIGN > **PROGRAM EXECUTION** > **TECH STACK**

Resourcing and coverage that supports GTM motion and complexity.

Campaigns and deliverables that enable customers, partners, and successful executions of GTM initiatives.

Enabling platforms and tools that drive engagement, productivity, analytics, and insights.

Depending on the size of your portfolio, you might consider creating a GTM center of excellence by establishing shared learning across your investment companies and giving them all access to a best practice playbook. Your bird's-eye view of what's working and what's not working across your portfolio will prove invaluable to the teams you've invested in.

**Just make sure the CEO owns
the GTM process.**

➡

According to Kelly, "For investors, [GTM] is about outcomes, not outputs." In other words, investors are less concerned about the activities being carried out (the outputs) than they are about the ROI, and they see GTM accordingly.

For the CEO trying to balance growth with softer but equally important things like investments in brand and culture, this pressure can become a bit of a problem. Since most investors are primarily concerned with creating ROI, they often push growth at all costs no matter what maturity stage the company is at.

If you're an investor, you probably worry about your portfolio of companies much of the time, but you can wind up trying to solve the wrong problem at the wrong business stage. Make sure that your guidance is aligned with the business maturity stage of each portfolio company respectively and make sure your metrics are aligned with that stage.

When a company is in the ideation stage, it's imperative for the CEO to prioritize getting to problem-market fit. Expecting them to perform on KPIs from the next stage (e.g., efficiency metrics) will force them to implement structure, which may hinder them from finding their ideal customer profile. Improving gross margins and nailing customer retention will come later. For now, apply the metrics that we laid out in the GTM maturity chapter. In doing so, you will ensure that you are pushing the CEO to measure success correctly based on their business stage.

Once you've reached the transition stage and you shift from problem-market fit to product-market fit, you will be pursuing growth more aggressively. Even then, you can't push growth at all costs. Rather, you need to achieve effective growth at scale, which includes building marquee accounts and investing in brand and culture with thought leadership to dominate their category—all of which will be essential to scale the company.

Investors should guide and shepherd CEOs and avoid a "growth at all costs" mentality.

CHIEF EXECUTIVE OFFICERS: THE OWNER

If you're the CEO, we implore you with every fiber of our being: *Take ownership of GTM!* Maybe you didn't realize this is something you need to own. You think of GTM as an execution, and you've got people to do that for you.

Well, it's time to change your perspective on GTM.

CEOs, GTM is *your* burden to bear! Own it!

Remember, it starts with an aligned executive team that has a shared understanding, KPIs, and data: a single source of truth. It's your job as CEO to create that alignment and get all of your executives operating at the same business stage with the same MOVE framework. It's also your job to work with each leader so you can figure out how to adapt their metrics as you grow through maturity stages.

We can summarize your role in this way:

The CEO's role in GTM is
alignment **and** *transformation.*

In practice, GTM winds up being delegated to other leaders. However, it's rarely clear *which* leaders, so ownership becomes vague. An ambiguity develops between company strategy and GTM process, and this is where things break down.

Doesn't it make your head hurt just trying to sort it all out?

So, to be clear, according to our research and despite their claims to the contrary, CEOs own the corporate strategy that drives GTM, but they rarely own the GTM process.

This dynamic needs to change!

One CEO who gets it, Nick Mehta from Gainsight, called GTM "an end-to-end process of how vendors help buyers along the customer journey." Nick takes a very active role in guiding GTM across his exec team. As we quoted earlier, Brian Halligan, CEO of HubSpot, said, "GTM is like a product."

As he explained, "We're obsessive about making the product better. We're the same way in our go-to-market . . . We're constantly asking, 'What are the bugs in it? What are customers complaining about in regard to their experience with our teams and processes? What features (GTM improvements) are they requesting?' We treat go-to-market like a product, and we track bugs and make improvements."

We treat go-to-market like a product, and we track bugs and make improvements.

Often, we find that CEOs have gotten their companies to a certain point in their growth because they knew what to do, but now they've reached a plateau. They don't know what move to make next. They aren't sure where the next summit is located.

"How do we increase the size and value of our company?"

They may be doing fine today, but what about next quarter? Next year?

If they can't answer the four questions of the MOVE framework (who, what, when, and where), then they may wind up executing the wrong thing.

CEOs want to build a business model that will keep adding new revenue streams: acquiring, expanding, going wider, entering new categories and markets. You can't do that if you don't have happy customers, and CEOs know this. So creating happy customers tends to be their primary focus.

Just beware, CEOs are often focused on strategy but not the <u>alignment</u> + <del>of</del> <u>execution</u> of that strategy. ≡ GTM

They may fail to select a GTM champion or align other leaders to a centralized GTM function, which means leaders wind up operating in silos.

If you're a CEO in the *ideation* stage, your job is to make sure the problem you're trying to solve is real enough, and the market big enough, for your solution. You won't have a perfect product at this point, and that's okay.

Once you reach the *transition* stage, your job is to align your entire organization around the product you're selling and the market you're going after. It's equally important to declare the top priorities and identify the things *not* to do. One common trap for companies at this stage is holding on to opportunities presented by multiple enticing segments. Like a tax on every activity, this will drain your team of energy, as well as water down the product experience and marketing message. If you have more than one great segment, pick one and grow it before you expand to the others.

By the time you get to the *expansion* stage, where you have multiple product lines, you may have multiple general managers for each of those product lines. You still need to create alignment among your general managers, treating them like mini-CEOs so you can help them deliver excellence and create a frictionless experience for customers.

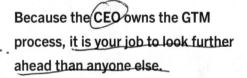

Because the CEO owns the GTM process, it is your job to look further ahead than anyone else.

Unfortunately, this is often a cause of misalignment. The CEO is thinking about the next big acquisition, while the rest of the team is focused on fixing problems for existing customers. The CEO might be thinking about opening an office in a new market where they see tremendous opportunity, while the team is still focused on the here and now. It becomes very easy for the CEO to introduce a lot of chaos into the company.

Therefore, you have to *yet,* **prioritize the alignment of your entire company.** (A. seqvel)

Learn to recognize when your company is approaching a moment of transformation so you can create alignment, change incentives, and put your executive team to work making the transformation happen.

"What got us *here* won't get us *there!*"

That's the message when it's time to transform. Use the maturity curve we presented earlier in the book to help you navigate the changes. It will provide you with a firm foundation as you create alignment because it clarifies the metrics you need to talk about during each stage of transformation.

Communication is key, but you have to start planting seeds for those big changes long before you announce your big decision. That way, when you decide to open that Berlin-to-Oslo route for your airline, it won't be a shock to the system for your entire company.

RevOps is going to become your best friend in all of this because they will enable you to act on better data (and a stable single source of truth). You no longer have to juggle different metrics from different teams and try to make them all add up somehow.

Yes, CEOs also use their instincts, intuition, and judgment to lead, but it's important to have data and predictability so the whole team can work in cadence.

Misaligned data = misaligned teams. Fix the data and you will align your teams.

Above all, remember, as CEO, you own GTM! Don't delegate it, even in a public company. Make RevOps your best friend as early as possible, regardless of the stage of your business, and work toward alignment and transformation for your entire company.

CHIEF MARKETING OFFICERS: THE GALVANIZER

In the world of GTM, CMOs need to be thinking about revenue above all else. It needs to be on the same shelf, if not slightly higher, than sales numbers. After all, GTM is about creating a high-performance revenue team, and you're trading in the old sales funnels for a revenue flywheel.

You should be thinking about revenue constantly. In the last fifteen to twenty years, marketing has been intensely focused on lead generation, so when we asked CMOs who they believe should take ownership of GTM, most of them said the chief revenue officer (CRO).

As the logic goes, since the CRO is the sales leader and therefore the "owner" of hitting the numbers, they must also be in charge of GTM.

Megan Eisenberg, CMO of TripActions, defined GTM in this way: "We have an overall company vision, mission, and strategy, then we have goals that we're trying to accomplish. Go-to-market is the execution against one or two of those goals, depending on if its product-related or revenue targets."

Focus more on building ideal customer profiles because you're going to play a big role in the M of the MOVE framework.

Account-based marketing will help you think at a customer segment level, which will then help you think at a customer cohort level, rather than just bringing in unidentified, unfiltered leads. It's a true partnership with the CRO.

As a CMO, there's a good chance you were brought in to help take your company from the ideation stage to the transition stage. Ideation is typically sales-focused and founder-led, but as the company moves toward the transition stage, they need to create strong sales and marketing alignment, which is why the partnership with the CRO is so important.

Make sure you are balancing marketing across the entire revenue pipeline, not just the top of the funnel.

Or you may be there to take the company to the execution stage, in which case, you need to begin thinking about customer advocacy and cohorts. Whatever the case, just remember, as CMO, you're there to move the company forward, so be intentional in your messaging, positioning, and differentiation.

Align your messaging throughout your organization so everyone is saying the same thing to the customer.

Don't leave this to chance because alignment almost never happens without intentionality. As part of creating GTM alignment, your marketing ops function will have to move under RevOps. Why? Because you can't have marketing ops functioning in a silo. RevOps is creating that single source of truth for the high-performing revenue team.

CHIEF REVENUE OFFICERS: THE ORCHESTRATOR

To get right to the point, the role of the CRO needs to be reimagined.

In addition to driving sales, CROs must now take charge of the customer success team.

Indeed, many companies have already made this shift, putting CROs in charge of both sales *and* customer success in order to go to market more effectively. We agree with this approach, as it contributes more effectively to creating that full-revenue flywheel.

Instead of dealing with separate, and sometimes contradictory, marketing, sales, and customer success numbers, you will have one revenue number to help you make smart decisions about top-line growth, such as how to bring in the right kinds of customers so you can retain them on the backend, whom to hire in order to hit goals, and so on.

The change from only owning sales to owning revenue is a big one, but it contributes to the alignment of your teams, which is at the heart of GTM transformation. Does that mean you still bear the burden of locking down the numbers each month and each quarter? Yes, you have to make short-term decisions to close out each quarter, but if you build predictability into your business through GTM transformation, then you can worry less about the short term and spend more time thinking strategically about the long term.

You're more likely to hit the numbers when you have a RevOps team as your foundation because of that single, centralized source of data. Just beware of the temptation to focus so hard on sales that you fail to align with the other teams.

> *You're more likely to hit the numbers*
> *when you have a RevOps team*
> *as your foundation.*

So, to summarize:

4 Key Stakeholders and their roles in their GTM process

	Investors	CEO	CMO	CRO
What's your role in GTM?	**You are the guide.** Create Centers of excellence and share best practices, benchmarks, and GTM playbooks relevant to the business stage.	**You are the owner.** Transform and align executive team with incentives and KPI's across the 3 business stages.	**You are the galvanizer.** Create a consistent brand experience across the buyer journey.	**You are the orchestrator.** Deliver a connected customer experience from sale to success.
What keeps you up at night around GTM?	• Is the market big enough? • How scalable is the GTM motion? • Do they have the right team?	• What moves will help transform our company to the next business stage? • How do we create single source of truth? • How to make trade-offs between growth, retention and new bets?	• Is our brand positioning us as a leader? • Is marketing creating fuel for sales? • How are we turning customers into advocates?	• How repeatable is our sales motion? • How do we forecast more accurately? • Are we creating long-term customers?
What will make your job easier?	Coach CEO through the 3Ps of the business stages. Create a peer mentoring program to help portfolio companies navigate the ups and downs of growth.	Make revenue ops your best friend. Combine sales and customer success into one revenue organization.	Make CRO & CFO your best friends. Turn your lead funnel into a revenue flywheel.	Create multiple ways to hit your number (acquisition, retention, expansion). Make marquee customers wildly successful and promote their story.

NOW YOU'RE READY TO GROW

By now, you should have an understanding of the basics of the MOVE framework and the role each key stakeholder needs to play. You know how to orchestrate your next move regardless of the stage, size, or complexity of your business. You know enough to begin finding your own answers to who, what, when, and where.

To implement the MOVE framework, overlay it with the information about your business maturity stage (ideation, transition, expansion), because that's going to determine the focus and shape of your GTM process.

The Three Stages and the 3Ps of GTM Business Transformation

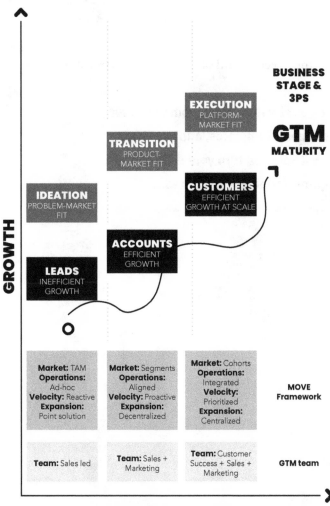

GROWTH (vertical axis)

TRANSFORMATION (horizontal axis)

BUSINESS STAGE & 3PS

EXECUTION
PLATFORM-MARKET FIT

TRANSITION
PRODUCT-MARKET FIT

GTM MATURITY

IDEATION
PROBLEM-MARKET FIT

CUSTOMERS
EFFICIENT GROWTH AT SCALE

ACCOUNTS
EFFICIENT GROWTH

LEADS
INEFFICIENT GROWTH

Market: TAM
Operations: Ad-hoc
Velocity: Reactive
Expansion: Point solution

Market: Segments
Operations: Aligned
Velocity: Proactive
Expansion: Decentralized

Market: Cohorts
Operations: Integrated
Velocity: Prioritized
Expansion: Centralized

MOVE Framework

Team: Sales led

Team: Sales + Marketing

Team: Customer Success + Sales + Marketing

GTM team

Once you do that, you should know exactly what your next step needs to be in order to get your fleet of airplanes flying higher, faster, and farther more reliably. From a single rickety flying machine launching off the end of a ramp, you've created a global airline taking customers to more places and providing a better and better experience.

That's the sweet reward of GTM business transformation.

Check out themovebook.com to download assessment, templates, and workbooks that will help you turn your GTM silos into a high-performing revenue team.

PUTTING THE MOVE FRAMEWORK INTO ACTION

NOW COMES THE FUN PART. YOU CAN START TODAY by putting the MOVE framework into action. We want to make this super simple for you, so we've created a number of templates that will help you assess exactly where you are on the maturity curve and figure out exactly what you need to do in order to transform for the next stage.

It's easy to get overwhelmed by all of the things you need to do in order to transform your organization. Indeed, the reason why companies get stuck is because they don't know what to measure, how to get their teams aligned, or what questions to ask.

The following templates can be used as an internal playbook to get your executive team on the same page.

In Section Two, we gave you everything you need to know to determine where you are on the maturity curve, as well as what it will take to progress to the next stage. Then, in Section Three, we gave you the MOVE framework, which provides three key questions for figuring out your next step.

The following templates gives you some strategic questions you can ask at the highest level. Knowing where you are on the GTM maturity curve is the first step to getting "unstuck" and taking your next step forward as a company, so we begin with a self-assessment. Bring your teams together and walk through the following exercise to figure out where you are right now.

THE GO-TO-MARKET ASSESSMENT

1) Which of these most accurately represents the **stage** of your business?

    a. **Ideation:** We are testing our hypotheses of the problem that we believe can be solved by the solution we are still building for the customers we have and the customers we believe are out there (likely less than $20 million in revenue).

b. **Transition:** We have a product with a cohort of happy customers, and we are looking to capture market share and gain or maintain a leadership position in our category (likely between $10 and $150 million in revenue).

c. **Execution:** Our potential to grow through existing customers far exceeds net new business, and we are developing new solutions and offerings to solve more of their problems and expand into new categories (likely around $100 million or higher in revenue).

2) What **metrics** are most important to your business now? In other words, what stuff keeps you up at night?

a. **Metrics by Function:** CPL, MQLs, outbound KPIs, meetings booked, Opp creation, funnel conversion rates, closed won revenue

b. **Metrics by Segments:** Performance by segments: engaged accounts, pipeline coverage, deal velocity, ACV, CAC, GRR, magic number

c. **Metrics by Customer Cohorts:** NRR, expansion, LTV, gross margins, multiproduct expansion

3) Which of the following best describes how you decide whom you should currently **market** to?

a. **TAM:** Anyone within a loosely defined TAM (total addressable market).

b. **Account Segments:** We have prioritized segments of named accounts that are coordinated across marketing channels and sales assignments.

c. **Customer Cohorts:** The majority of our revenue/growth must come from existing customers rather than from new logo acquisition.

4) Which of the following best describes how your company determines what it needs to **operate** effectively?

a. **Ad Hoc:** Department-level data and opinions with the authority to make decisions.

b. **Aligned:** Shared assessment of the data and aligned decision making across sales and marketing with dedicated ops for each department.

c. **Integrated:** Coordinated decision making across GTM teams led by a centralized RevOps team aligned to achieve company objectives using shared systems, data, processes, and an executive performance scorecard.

5) Which of the following best describes your company's approach to knowing when it's time to scale (**velocity**)?

a. **Reactive** to the needs of each department: "There's a fire, so we hire someone to put it out."

b. **Proactive** to the needs of each department: "Invest now to prevent future fires."

c. **Prioritized** across GTM teams to achieve company goals: "Invest for growth, not for pain."

6) Which of the following best describes where you can **expand** the most in the near term?

a. **Single-threaded expansion:** One distribution path (direct, agency, or partner)

b. **Partial expansion:** Additional distribution paths and coverage areas (GEOs, verticals)

c. **Full expansion:** Multiple products toward becoming a platform

Once you know where you are on the GTM maturity curve, you can begin strategizing your next move. The following templates provide high-level strategic questions for the MOVE framework at every stage of the maturity curve.

Go-to-Market Templates and Questions to Transform Your Business

If you're at the *ideation* stage, your focus should be on *problem-market fit*, determining whether the problem you're trying to solve with your solution provides enough market opportunity for growth and success. Don't worry if you can't answer the *transition* or *execution* questions yet. There's no reason to jump the gun. In fact, you *shouldn't* know all of the answers to the questions in this section yet. Focus on problem-market fit for now until you nail it. Only then will you be ready to move on to the next stage.

Once you have clarity around the problem you're going to solve and you've created a solution that you're ready to take to market, it's time to make the move from *ideation* to *transition*. At this stage, your focus changes from problem-market fit to product-market fit, as your marketing and sales teams get aligned on what needs to happen. The *transition* template will help with that alignment by providing clarity around the segments that your account-based team needs to be going after. Again, don't worry about answering the *execution* questions at this point.

When you have multiple products in the market with integrated RevOps, you're at the *execution* stage. Now you're focused on *platform-marketing fit* and growth potential, and you should be able to answer all of the questions in the following templates.

These are the questions you need to discuss with your team in order to work through your strategic, alignment, and transformation challenges, using the MOVE framework as a guide to help you clarify your next move.

IDEATION STAGE—PROBLEM-MARKET FIT

Market

Strategic questions:

- What problem are you solving?
- How big is your market?
- How are you positioned?

Alignment questions:

- Who is your buyer?
- What size of company and verticals are you having the most success with?
- Which territories are you focusing on?
- Which use cases are working the best?

Transformation questions:

- What's stopping you from creating repeatable sales motions?
- What changes in market approach would speed up market adoption?

Operations

Strategic questions:

- What KPIs are you looking at to see if there is a problem-market fit?
- How are you incentivizing teams to deliver on these KPIs?

Alignment questions:

- What tech is helping each of your GTM teams to deliver business outcomes?
- How do marketing, sales, and finance operations teams align on common definitions and KPIs?

Transformation questions:

- What's stopping you from focusing on your best-fit accounts over lead funnels?
- How quickly can you look at all operational metrics across GTM functions to make business decisions?

Velocity

Strategic questions:

- How is your sales force trained and iterating on the product pitch?
- How quickly is your sales team hitting quota, and how quickly is marketing creating more demand?

Alignment questions:

- Is there a team (one or more) dedicated to training sales hires and providing ongoing support?
- How are you tracking and testing ramp ratios for sales ramp to quota, marketing ramp to demand gen, SDR ramp to pipeline, and customer to ROI?

Transformation questions:

- What's stopping you from creating higher velocity in your ramp ratios?
- What would you need to know to hire proactively?

Expansion

Strategic questions:

- How are you selling? Direct, channels, partners, agencies?
- What percentage of your revenue is coming from each distribution type?

Alignment questions:

- What distribution type should you focus on?
- How quickly can you test new distribution channels?

Transformation questions:

- What's stopping you from going in different industries, verticals, geographies?
- Should you be going upmarket or downmarket?
- How do you increase your average deal size?

TRANSITION STAGE—PRODUCT-MARKET FIT

Market

Strategic questions:

- What segments are your best performing and why?
- Can you replicate that success into other segments?
- What new use cases would drive up your deal size?

Alignment questions:

- How is your GTM team aligning around segments?
- How do you align your messaging and value proposition for each segment across GTM touchpoints?
- How are you going from TAM to TRM to further prioritize within each segment?

Transformation questions:

- How will you achieve top ranking in analysts for your key category?
- What's stopping you from selling similar solutions to similar buyer for similar problems at scale?

Operations

Strategic questions:

- What KPIs are you looking at to see if there is a product-market fit?
- How are you adjusting the incentives of leaders and teams to deliver on the new KPIs?

Alignment questions:

- How predictable are your conversion metrics?
- How are you balancing the tradeoffs between retention and acquisition?

Transformation questions:

- What's stopping you from creating a single source of truth?
- How are your tools across GTM teams integrated to help you generate better business insights?

Velocity

Strategic questions:

- What are your highest priority velocity ramps (*people* and *enablement*) that need improvement?
- What key leadership hires are needed to add new functions and scale your organization?

Alignment questions:

- How are you coordinating training, documentation, kickoffs, and release launch schedules across the GTM team and customers?
- How are you making holistic hiring decisions to support your highest priorities rather than the needs of departments?

Transformation questions:

- What's stopping you from aligning enablement functions across departments?
- What changes do you need to make to deliver a unified experience to your customers?

Expansion

Strategic questions:

- How quickly can you expand into different industries, verticals, or geographies?
- What new products or services will your existing customers happily pay for to solve their problems?

Alignment questions:

- How would your business model shift if you went upmarket or downmarket?
- What makes your product sticky?

Transformation questions:

- What's stopping you from having the biggest deals with your top customers?
- What's stopping you from adding pro-serves to increase deal size?
- What percentage of your revenue is coming from each coverage area?

EXECUTION STAGE—PLATFORM-MARKET FIT

Market

Strategic questions:

- What additional problems could you solve to expand your value for existing customers?
- Which build, buy, or partner approach(es) will ensure you can scale growth?
- Who are your competitors today versus tomorrow, and how will you transition for this?

Alignment questions:

- How do you sequence your "land and expand" offering?
- How will you identify customers who are ready for expansion opportunities?

Transformation questions:

- Which adjacent categories should you move into?
- How are your customers helping you redefine the new North Star?

Operations

Strategic questions:

- What KPIs are you looking at to see if there is a platform-market fit?
- How are you adjusting the incentives of leaders and teams to deliver on the new KPIs?

Alignment questions:

- How do you create, maintain, and communicate a common GTM scorecard?
- How do you proactively look at churn and growth to address them before it's too late?
- What data do you need to consistently review and deliver on business forecasts?

Transformation questions:

- What new products and services do you need to keep growing with your existing base?
- Which new markets can you test to open new opportunities?

Velocity

Strategic questions:

- How do you create and enable new lines of business?
- How do you keep the customer at the center of every process?

Alignment questions:

- What are the key hires (e.g., business line general managers, GEO executives) to support platform growth or global expansion?
- How frequently and seamlessly does your GTM enablement team work to create and deliver employee onboarding, bootcamps, certification, decks, playbooks, and quarterly business reviews?

Transformation questions:

- What's stopping you from creating centers of excellence and benchmarking ramps and making investments toward even bigger growth?

Expansion

Strategic questions:

- Which channels can you invest in for nonlinear growth?
- How do you create and enable new lines of businesses?

Alignment questions:

- What percentage of your revenue is coming from each line of business?
- How do you prioritize new product releases, budgets, and resources across multiple products?
- What percentage of revenue is coming from customers versus net new customers?

Transformation questions:

- What will it take to create the top ten biggest deals in your category with your platform + multiyear + precommit + pro-serve attachment rate?
- What percentage of your revenue is coming from $100,000 deals?

Finally, the big question:

WHAT WILL BE YOUR NEXT MOVE?

Check out themovebook.com
to download assessment, templates,
and workbooks that will help you turn
your GTM silos into a high-performing
revenue team.

CONCLUSION

BY NOW, YOU SHOULD BE ABLE TO IDENTIFY THE
stage your business is at, you should have a good idea what your
GTM focus needs to be, and what your team should look like
according to the MOVE framework. Let's take a final look at each
of these things so you will leave here with a clear understanding
of what you need to do.

First of all, don't try to get it all done right away. We didn't bring
you to this point just so you would feel overwhelmed by everything you have to do. On the contrary, all you need to worry about
right now is understanding what your focus is supposed to be and
making sure you nail it. You can then use the strategic, alignment,
and transformation questions we provided to determine your
next move.

All you need to worry about right now is
understanding what your focus is supposed
to be and making sure you nail it.

Let's assume for a moment that you're the CEO of a company in the ideation stage. What is all of this supposed to look like for you? Let's take it one stage at a time.

In the ideation stage, you're still figuring out if the market is big enough for the problem you're trying to solve. Most likely, your GTM focus will be lead generation, and you'll have a sales leader directing that process.

When you apply the MOVE framework at this stage, it's going to be quite broad. In other words, your *market* will consist of whomever you can get to listen to you as you test your hypothesis. Your *operations* will probably be very ad hoc, working at a departmental level, as you make quick, imperfect decisions.

The *velocity* of getting things done will be reactive because you're trying new things to see what works and you're putting out fires as they appear. In terms of *expansion*, you're probably single-threaded. You may have anywhere from a one-person to a few-dozen-person sales team. Your KPIs are focused on things like cost-per-lead, booking numbers, and your highest conversion rate from the top of the funnel. You may be tracking a lot of activities that happen in marketing and sales, but you have inefficient growth.

By the way, all of that is okay for the ideation stage of your business.

To close out our flying metaphor, your airline company isn't off the ground yet. You're on the runway, making sure everything works so you know the airplane is ready to fly. And that's perfectly fine. In fact, that's exactly where you should be at this point.

As you move from ideation to transition, you now have product-market fit, which means your product is performing well for an addressable market you can keep selling into. Your airplane is off the ground, offering regular service for customers to a couple of key cities and trying to grow that customer base. By now, you probably have a lot more sales and customer success reps, and you're working to build out the senior leadership across departments, even scaling the marketing team to run ABM and support the sales pipeline. Instead of focusing on leads, you now have a target list of accounts to go after.

When you apply the MOVE framework at this stage, you're narrowing that broad *market* focus to pursue customer segments. Your *operations* is going to align sales and marketing, as they focus on the top accounts they want to focus on. Consequently, your *velocity* is going to shift from reactive to proactive, and you may even test some *expansion*.

You might even be able to go into multiple locations or verticals (Is it time for that Berlin to Oslo route?). Metrics revolve around answering questions like, "How do we increase our deal size? How can we close more deals in this market faster?" You're using more efficiency metrics as well, such as trying to get a better cost per acquisition, as you create a scalable, repeatable model.

Once you move into the execution stage, you now have platform-market fit, with more than one product that you can potentially sell—and in multiple markets. At this stage, customer success becomes super critical. Instead of leads or accounts, you're looking at customers as the base where you can sell your new products and services. That's your most important market for growth. You're closing more deals within your customer base, increasing the value of your deal size with accounts you've already sold to. They're no longer random accounts but customer cohorts that you can segment in different ways.

In terms of operations, you have a dedicated RevOps team giving you a single source of truth that allows you to make accurate decisions faster. When it comes to velocity, you're proactive, prioritizing which markets you're going after, which products to sell, and which business lines will work best.

You're able to take big steps into expansion, with more channels, possibly more product lines, selling in different regions. You may have APIs, partner programs, and agencies so you can now focus on figuring out where to grow the most. The KPIs that matter are things like CLV. How much revenue can you generate from each product line? What's your NPS score? What is your net revenue retention? Indeed, what you're doing at this point is creating efficient growth at scale, and happy successful customers become the life blood of the business.

Your airline now offers more routes to more places, a better customer experience, and maybe additional services, and you're constantly looking for the best place to expand flights to new cities. This is the stage where enduring companies are made, the kind that change the world and that are tracked in financial markets. They've gained the ability to continuously transform and grow. In fact, the very reason we named the last stage *execution* is because it suggests an unstoppable movement, and that's what these companies have.

That's an overview of what we've shared with you in this book. Remember, it's okay to be at whatever stage you're at. Our goal is to help you focus on the right thing for your stage so you can nail it. That way, you can get ready to move to the next stage.

Remember, it's okay to be at
whatever stage you're at.

But let's make it even easier. Here is the essence of the entire book in a single chart:

MOVE Framework

Business Stage & the 3Ps / GTM Focus & the team	Ideation Problem-market fit	Transition Product-market fit	Execution Platform-market fit
	Leads Sales-led	**Accounts** Sales & Marketing	**Customers** Customer Success + Sales + Marketing
1. Market (who) Who should we market to?	**TAM** Broad - minimal prioritization	**Segments** Relevant accounts (TRM + ICP + Intent)	**Cohorts** Customer cohorts + Relevant new accounts
2. Operations (what) What do you need to operate effectively?	**Ad-hoc** Department level data and decision making authority	**Aligned** Shared understanding of the data and aligned decision making with dedicated ops for each department	**RevOps** Coordinated decision making a cross GTM teams aligned to achieve company objectives led by centralized rev ops team using shared systems, data, processes and GTM scorecard
3. Velocity (when) When can we scale our business?	**Reactive** When there's a fire, hire someone to put it out	**Proactive** Invest now to prevent future fires	**Prioritized** Invest for growth not for pain
4. Expansion (where) Where can we grow the most?	**Single threaded expansion** One distribution path (direct, channel or partner)	**Partial expansion** Multiple distribution paths and coverage areas (GEOs, Verticals)	**Full expansion** Distribution + Coverage + Multiple products, platform, & ecosystem
KPI's	**Metrics by functions** Funnel Conv rates, CPL Bookings & Win rate Sales activities (calls, demo's, ops) Marketing activities (traffic, leads)	**Metrics by account segments** Engagement Pipeline coverage Deal velocity Average deal size, GRR Efficiency metrics (magic number, CAC)	**Metrics by customer cohorts** CLV, Time to value, NPS, Customer ROI Product line revenue & Pipeline NRR / Net Expansion Gross Margins Growth by category
Business Outcomes	Inefficient growth	Efficient growth	Efficient growth at scale

You now have what you need to make your next move, so all you have to do is implement it. Put the MOVE framework into action in your company.

We're here for you, visit themovebook.com if you have additional questions or want help from our team on your own GTM transformation. We also want to provide you with plenty of resources for further study, so we've created a comprehensive list of podcasts, websites, and influencers who can help you with GTM transformation.

You can do this! Ask the right questions, get better answers, and take your company into the future with confidence.

Check out themovebook.com to download assessment, templates, and workbooks that will help you turn your GTM silos into a high-performing revenue team.

RESOURCES
FOR GO-TO-MARKET

FROM BORING2BORING
TO BONUS2BONUS

A LOT OF AMAZING PEOPLE AND A LOT OF AMAZING companies have navigated the difficult corridors of the GTM transformation journey. If you've been struggling, you're certainly not alone. Although we've provided you with a simple framework to help you answer the key questions of GTM, we know a whole lot of smart, experienced people who are contributing to the conversation in mind-blowing ways.

As you move forward aligning your teams and identifying your next best opportunity, we want to give you plenty of additional resources. Remember, GTM is an iterative process, which means you should always be thinking of ways to improve it. To that end, we have compiled a list of people, authors, and podcasts that we strongly encourage you to check out. They're going to help you on your GTM transformation journey so you, too, can achieve amazing things and soar ever higher.

WEBSITE RESOURCES

You can begin with this website we've created for the book. There was simply no way we could share all of the content we've put together about GTM transformation in a single book, so we've compiled a breathtaking amount of information for even deeper dives on every aspect of the MOVE framework.

You can find it at **themovebook.com**.

For more personalized one-on-one advice, feel free to reach out to us. We stand ready to guide you through the intricacies of GTM transformation no matter where you are on the GTM maturity curve.

THE TOP GO-TO-MARKET
PODCASTS

The following GTM podcasts provide ongoing advice, encouragement, and tips for creating and improving your iterative GTM process. Many of them have already accumulated an impressive library of podcast episodes that you can wade through. We've included helpful descriptions of each podcast so you can find the ones that are most relevant to your needs.

Brian Halligan, CEO of HubSpot, "Pivoting from a Startup Leader to a Scale-up Leader w/Brian Halligan" (Episode 296)

A scaling-up company leader needs to shed his startup skin and reemerge as a whole new animal. How? In the following ways: Let the experts you hired make their best decisions. Make your major changes in the startup phase. Regardless of industry, tech's holy grail has an enterprise back end and consumer-friendly front end. The leader sets the tone and makes the big-picture decisions. Make your product easy to buy and use—no exceptions. Make a plan, prioritize, and stick with it. https://open.spotify.com/episode/5wkHcaAWQqcKykUzZJLsjh?si=Bzg9thqaSnuYz4uRiAT0tg

John Ellett, CEO of Springbox, "CMOs Build Trust with the Customer and the C-Suite" (Episode 710)

With so many C-suite acronyms flying around, it's hard to keep track of what each one does. Luckily, you can always ask an expert. Which is why we're diving into the role of the CMO with John Ellett, CEO at Springbox and contributor at *Forbes* CMO Network. https://podcasts.apple.com/us/

podcast/710-cmos-build-trust-with-the-customer-the-c-suite/id1155
097337?i=1000493596328

David Lewis, Partner/Principal of BDO Digital, "What It Takes to Write a Book" (Episode 709)

You don't have to be a writer to write a book. Do you have something to say? Are you knowledgeable on a certain topic that the majority of the world may not be? Then maybe you should write a book. David Lewis (DemandGen) and Sangram Vajre (Terminus) have each written books to create credibility in their space, and it has been a game changer for their businesses. They gathered their insight, personal experiences, and all the content they'd already created in the past and built their books, then they let editors do the rest. So what does it take to get your book done? David and Sangram take us through everything you should consider. https:// podcasts.apple.com/us/podcast/709-what-it-takes-to-write-a-book/id1155097337?i=1000493328282

Greg Segall, CEO/Founder of Alyce, "Flip the Script on Gifting to Make More Personal Connections" (Episode 705)

Why do we still send swag with our companies' names on it? We should all be a little more personal with our gifts. What better way than to let people choose their own? That's exactly what Greg Segall, CEO and founder at Alyce, decided to do. His approach to creating personal experiences is changing gifting forever. In this episode, he discusses why personal—not personalized—gifts are the future, how to turn a "touch" into a moment, and how to let your prospect create permission. https://podcasts.apple.com/us/podcast/705-gifting-better-how-to-move-from-personalized-to/id1155097337?i=1000493026128

Bob Conlin, CEO of NAVEX Global, "CMO to CEO—How Marketing Leaders Can Make the Ultimate Transition" (Episode 422)

There are several steadfast qualities that make a great leader. Are those traits inherent in a leader, or are they learned? The answer: both. FMF guest host Katie Bullard had the chance to discuss the qualities of a great leader with NAVEX Global's CEO, Bob Conlin. In this episode, they cover the top qualities of a great CEO, aligning with the long-term goals of your company, and more. https://podcasts.apple.com/gh/podcast /686-cmo-to-ceo-how-marketing-leaders-can-make-ultimate/id1155 097337?i=1000489717746

Brett Hagler, CEO/Co-founder of New Story, "New Story Charity— What to Say When Things Go Bad: Good!" (Episode 680)

What do you do when things go bad? Try saying, "Good!" Every crisis hides an opportunity; you just need to find it. So says Brett Hagler, CEO at New Story, a charity whose mission is to pioneer solutions to end global homelessness. In this episode, Brett covers why in a crisis you should make something people really want, you should do things that don't scale, and you should find opportunities. https://podcasts.apple. com/us/podcast/680-the-opportunities-hidden-behind-every-crisis/ id1155097337?i=1000489180011

Ryan Deiss, Founder/CEO of DigitalMarketer, "The Next Big Thing in B2B Is the Newsletter" (Episode 565)

It always amazes us when old things make a comeback. Whether it's the music you liked when you were a kid, questionable fashion choices (how many times are bell-bottoms coming back?), or '80s-nostalgia-fueled Netflix shows. It's happening in marketing, too. The next big thing in B2B goes all the way back to the beginning of online marketing: the email newsletter. In this episode, Ryan Deiss, CEO of DigitalMarketer and a competent juggler, explains why the email newsletter is having a renaissance right now, and how we can add it to our toolset. https:// listen.casted.us/public/6/The-FlipMyFunnel-Podcast-05659/608043e2

Kyle Lacy, Chief Marketing Officer of Lessonly, "What It Takes to Be a Modern CMO"

Modern CMOs wear a bunch of different hats, and that involves being an expert in several different fields. They have to be obsessed with the entire customer journey from prospect to upsell. They have to balance lead generation and brand management. And they have to measure results when they can, while simultaneously being comfortable investing in marketing activities that can't be measured. https://listen.casted.us/public/6/The-FlipMyFunnel-Podcast-05659/d8017f48

Kipp Bodnar, CMO of HubSpot, "How to Be a Kick-Ass CMO of an Iconic Brand" (Episode 696)

Have you ever wondered what it's like to be a CMO of a sales and marketing behemoth? We just got a pretty good idea of what it's like from HubSpot CMO Kipp Bodnar. What better place to catch up with Kipp than INBOUND 2019? https://podcasts.apple.com/ca/podcast/696-how-to-be-a-kick-ass-cmo-of-an-iconic-brand/id1155097337?i=1000491301578

Madison Bennett, Marketing Operations Lead of Marketo, "How to Practice Fearlessness in Marketing" (Episode 729)

Fearlessness is taking the keys to the Ferrari. That's one of our core values at Terminus, but what does it look like to be fearless in marketing?

Madison Bennett, marketing operations coordinator at Terminus, says it's about being unafraid to challenge people and processes at any turn. When it comes to marketing operations, you want the best accounts to be your customer. Period. When you find the best accounts for your sales team, that customer is going to flow through your deal cycle so much faster because you know they're ready to buy. They're also going to be better accounts for your customer success team to work with because they're engaged and interested in what you're doing. You have to be fearless in doing what it takes to find those key accounts for sales to go after and for customer success to engage. You have to find the best process for "teeing up" only the accounts that are going to be most successful. Whereas the goal used to be "fill that funnel" with as many people as possible, you now know exactly why you sent each account to sales. But how do you sustain fearlessness in marketing operations? https://podcasts. apple.com/us/podcast/729-how-to-practice-fearlessness-in-marketing/ id1155097337?i=1000497025861

Levi Ayriss/Lance Risser, VP of Southwest Field Operations at Dutch Bros. Coffee, "Build a Community by Making Customer Experience Your Mission" (Episode 726)

What is your mission? It may not seem like it, but your mission is the most important factor in delivering great customer experience. In this *Takeover* episode, host Ethan Beute speaks with Levi Ayriss, VP of southwest field operations, and Lance Risser, VP of field operations, at Dutch Bros. Coffee. https://podcasts.apple.com/us/podcast/726-build -community-by-making-customer-experience-your/id1155097337?i =1000496216499

Samantha Yarborough, Director of Strategic Partnerships at PFL, "Deliver Real-World Experience That Grabs Attention" (Episode 844)

Samantha Yarborough, Director of Strategic Partnerships at PFL. com, uses her decade of passionate marketing experience to help guide customers through their funnels effectively and quickly (regardless of where prospects may be), teaching them how to successfully execute tactile direct marketing campaigns. https://podcasts.apple.com/us/podcast/844-deliver-real-world-experience-that-grabs-attention/id1155097337?i=1000519465619

Henry Schuck, CEO and Co-founder of ZoomInfo, "How to Take a Company from $0 to $360 Million and Growing" (Episode 807)

During the economic volatility of the pandemic, we talked a lot about businesses downsizing or even shutting down their operations. It was easy to think things were hopeless, but what about the businesses who seized the opportunity to do big things? Like launching the biggest software IPO in a decade? That's exactly what Henry Schuck, CEO and co-founder at ZoomInfo, did. His story is not just a beacon of hope but also a how-to guide for taking a company from $0 to $360 million. https://podcasts.apple.com/us/podcast/807-how-to-take-a-company-from-%240-to-%24360-million-growing/id1155097337?i=1000512031625

Darryl Praill, CRO of VanillaSoft, "On the CMO Track: How to Become a CMO" (Episode 782)

He hasn't been a CMO just once. He's been a serial CMO at multiple successful companies. As a result, he's learned a little something about how to knock the role out of the park. That's where our guest on today's LinkedIn live episode is sitting: he's Darryl Praill, CRO at VanillaSoft and many-time CMO. First, he delivers a fire sales pitch and invites everyone listening to connect with him on LinkedIn. https://podcasts. apple.com/us/podcast/782-on-the-cmo-track-how-to-become-a-cmo/ id1155097337?i=1000506723447

Jay Abraham, CEO of The Abraham Group, Inc., "How the Highest-Paid Marketing Consultant Thinks Outside the Box" (Episode 770)

If you want to succeed, work hard. But if you want to be the best, you have to think outside the box. That's how Jay Abraham, CEO of The Abraham Group, became the highest-paid marketing consultant in the world. https://podcasts.apple.com/us/podcast/770-how-highest-paid-marketing-consultant-thinks-outside/ id1155097337?i=1000504422478

Jen Grant, CEO of Appify, "The Top 3 Priorities of a CMO Who Raised $103M with $1.6B in Valuation" (Episode 749)

Do you have a Department of Customer Love? Maybe that should be one of your marketing priorities this year. In this episode of the #FlipMyFunnel podcast, we spoke to Jen Grant about the culture at Looker, her top priorities as the CMO, and how account-based marketing is related to these priorities. https://podcasts.apple.com/us/ podcast/749-top-3-priorities-cmo-who-raised-%24103m-%241-6b-in/ id1155097337?i=1000501584062

Kirby Wadsworth, CMO of Ionir, "How a 4-Time CMO Says You Should Create Your Ideal Customer Profile"

ABM is easy as soon as you define your original ideal customer profile, but that's like the old Steve Martin answer on *How to Be a Millionaire*:

"First step: Get a million dollars." So how do you get that million dollars? Or, in this case, how do you define your ideal customer profile? Our advice, listen to this guy: Kirby Wadsworth. If that name seems familiar to you, it's because he's the author of an Amazon five-star book, was featured in *Forbes*'s "Most Influential CMOs on Social Media," and he's won tons of awards in the B2B space, including the Webby and W3 Awards and SiriusDecisions Return on Marketing & Sales Integration Award, to name a few. https://podcasts.apple.com/us/podcast /734-how-4-time-cmo-says-you-should-create-your-ideal/id115509 7337?i=1000497429498

Daniel Pink, *New York Times* Best-selling Author, "The Future of Work and Productivity" (Episode 700)

The world looks different in this crisis. How different will it look when it's all over? Will work ever work the same way again? In this episode, we catch up with the perfect person to answer these questions, Daniel Pink. Best-selling author of *To Sell Is Human* and host of *The Pinkcast*, Daniel has devoted the last twenty years to studying the intersection between science and work. We discuss why we need empathy in a crisis and why transparency matters right now. https:// podcasts.apple.com/us/podcast/700-the-future-of-work-productivity/ id1155097337?i=1000492082430

Ryan O' Hara, VP of Growth and Marketing at LeadIQ, "Aligning Sales and Marketing on the Same Content Map" (Episode 659)

More than ever, sales and marketing need to be on the same page and provide content. In this interview, Ryan O'Hara, VP of Growth and Marketing at LeadIQ, talks about alignment and content strategies that work for sales teams. https://podcasts.apple.com/us/podcast/659-aligning

-sales-and-marketing-on-the-same-content-map/id1155097337?i=
1000486241399

Katie Burke, Chief People Officer at HubSpot, "Think and Grow Rich Company Culture" (Episode 627)

In order to cultivate exceptional company culture, you need to think and grow rich. In this throwback episode, we sit down with Katie Burke, Chief People Officer of HubSpot, to talk about the importance of company culture. https://podcasts.apple.com/us/podcast/627-think-and-grow-rich-company-culture/id1155097337?i=1000477538676

Meagen Eisenberg, CMO of TripActions, and Ryan Bonnici, CMO of Whereby, "How CMOs Lead in Uncertain Times" (Episode 615)

Think about the most famous leaders in history. Were any of them known for leading through easy times? Responding to crises is what defines a leader. How will you respond? On the episode, we are joined by two incredible CMOs who have a ton of great tips for how you can better lead your marketing teams through this unprecedented time: Meagen Eisenberg and Ryan Bonnici. https://podcasts.apple.com/us/podcast/615-how-cmos-lead-in-uncertain-times/id1155097337?i=1000475666635

Jim Ewel, President and Founder of AgileMarketing.Net, "Why Experimenting Is the New Marketing" (Episode 592)

Question: If your company had forty events per year instead of one, would you improve as if you had forty years' worth of learning? This question is about the benefits of an iterative approach—one of the pillars of agile marketing. There's a lot of confusion about what agile marketing is, and many dismiss it as the latest buzzword. In this episode of #FlipMyFunnel, we're joined by Jim Ewel, former Vice-President of Marketing at Microsoft. Jim unpacks why iterative, goal-aligned experimentation is a superior strategy to large expensive campaigns. https://podcasts.apple. com/us/podcast/592-why-experimenting-is-the-new-marketing/id 1155097337?i=1000472497938

Michael Hyatt, Author and Former CEO of a $250 Million Publishing Company, "What It Takes to Become a Vision-Driven Leader" (Episode 590)

At what point in life did you realize you needed to start writing things down? We all eventually need to keep track of things, otherwise they slip through the cracks. Writing the little things down helps. What we schedule happens. So why don't we do that with the big things, too? Our dreams, our goals, our vision. Michael Hyatt, CEO of Michael Hyatt & Company and *New York Times* best-selling author of *The Vision-Driven Leader*, says we should. His book covers all of the ways we can shape ourselves into vision-driven leaders. The first step to accomplishing that vision? Writing it down. In the present tense. https://podcasts.apple. com/us/podcast/590-what-it-takes-to-become-a-vision-driven-leader/ id1155097337?i=1000472033786

Allen Gannett, Author of *The Creative Curve*, "The Creative Curve" (Episode 587)

According to our friend Allen Gannett, the CEO of TrackMaven and one of the keynote speakers at the very first #FlipMyFunnel conference, anybody can be a genius. Allen has written a book called *The Creative Curve* in which he explores the myth that we are born creative and explores how you, too, can be a creative genius. All it takes is a lot of hard work, a little

luck, and what Allen calls "The 4 Laws of the Creative Curve." https://
podcasts.apple.com/us/podcast/587-the-creative-curve/id1155097337
?i=1000471646933

Soon Yu, Best-selling Author of *Iconic Advantage*,
"Creating Meaningful Marketing in the B2B World" (Episode 568)

It isn't always the biggest, baddest, or fastest mousetrap that gets the mice.
It's the one with the stinkiest cheese. This translates directly to marketing, so says Soon Yu, author of *Iconic Advantage: Don't Chase the New,
Innovate the Old*. Soon helps companies realize that they don't have to be
the fastest, biggest, or have the best technology in order to be successful.
But they do have to connect with their audience, and the best way to
do that is through meaningful marketing. If there is no emotional con-
nection created with customers, they're just competing on price. There
aren't many winners in that game. In this episode of the #FlipMyFunnel
podcast, we chat with Soon about B2B storytelling, chasing the new
versus innovating the old, and three qualities behind the most successfully innovative and iconic companies. https://podcasts.apple.com/
us/podcast/568-creating-meaningful-marketing-in-the-b2b-world/
id1155097337?i=1000468855296

THE TOP GO-TO-MARKET
INFLUENCERS

There are many important voices in the world of GTM transformation, but we personally recommend these influencers. The people listed here are some of the smartest minds when it comes to GTM. Obviously, it's not possible to follow absolutely everyone. We all have limited time, so we recommend focusing on the individuals who are most relevant or interesting to you.

Emerging CMOs

- Kira Tchernikovsky, Co-founder of Customerization
- Lisa Sharapata, VP of Marketing, Brand, and Demand at MindTickle
- Mudassar Malik, VP of Marketing at mobileLIVE
- LingRaj Patil, CMO of Blue Marble
- Adam Hejna, Revenue Operations Leader at Kentico Kontent
- Corrina Owens, Director of Marketing, ABM, and Demand Generation at Profisee
- Benjamin Pope, Marketing Automation and ABM Manager at Corevist
- Tony A. Ramirez, VP of Economic Development at The Borderplex Alliance
- Avnita Gulati Sr., Director of Global Marketing Operations at Visa
- Jacob Rouser, Director of Digital Marketing and Demand Generation at Skience
- Tamara Kitić Yarovoy, Head of Demand Generation at Meltwater
- Heather Robinette, Director of Marketing at CertifID
- Tim Hillison, CMO Advisory at entrypoint1
- Dhriti Goyal, Head of Growth Marketing at Happay
- Udayan Belsare, Europe Marketing Lead at Mphasis
- Sarah Allen-Short, VP of Give and Take

- Jen Leaver, Senior Marketing Manager of Demand Generation and Global ABM at Bazaarvoice
- Leela Gill, VP of Marketing and Design at Intelligence Node
- Kate Hahn, Director of Global Demand Generation and Retention at Bazaarvoice
- Erin Grubbs, Director of Marketing Programs at GoReact
- Melissa Schaaf, Sr. Manager of Partner Marketing at Quantum Metric
- Becky Hobbs, Founder and Principal at Hobbscross
- Sara Haas, Head of Marketing at IMTC
- Torrey Dye, Director of ABM at Caroo
- Pete Lorenco, VP of Marketing at Avid
- Brittany Rolfe Hillard, VP of Customer Engagement and Advocacy at WalkMe
- David Hoeller, B2B Marketing Director at BlueVoyant
- Daniel Englebretson, Founder of Khronos
- Jamie Levy, Head of Merchant Engagement at Shopify Plus
- Odia Kalala-Shembo, Assistant Marketing Manager/Content Specialist at Commercial Credit Group Inc.
- Matt Shachter, Director of Marketing at Bungee Tech
- Rahul Mehta, Co-founder, CTO, and CPO of Exprs
- Chris Thompson, Head of Marketing Operations at Conga
- Julianna Meidell, VP of Marketing at Encamp
- Jake Stuart, Digital Marketing Manager at Bazaarvoice
- Angela Trapasso, Head of Growth Marketing at AuctionNinja
- Ankit Sharma, BMC Head of Account-Based Marketing at Netcore Solutions
- Lorena Morales, VP of Marketing at Go Nimbly
- Jess Gondolfo, Marketing Director at Synup
- Daniel Cowan, Director, Growth Marketing Beaver at Fit North America
- Julian Parr, Senior Manager of Marketing at DLT Labs
- Be'Anka Ashaolu, VP and Marketing at Propel

- Krista Drager, Marketing Manager at Sentry Equipment
- Chris Nichols, VP of Marketing at endevis
- Amber Bogie, ABM Strategist at Degreed
- Tyler Pleiss, Account-Based Marketing Manager—Strategic at Terminus
- Andy Mackensen, Co-founder and CMO at Caroo
- Vanessa Hershberger, Marketing Specialist at Alaska Communications
- Aya (Fawzy) Cockcroft, Director of Demand Generation at Ordr Inc.
- Cody Ward, Sr. Director of Demand Generation Marketing at Conexiom
- Amine Ammar, Director of Business Development at Avantage Industriel
- Abdul Rastagar, GTM Leader and Marketing Author
- Matthew Geise, VP of Marketing at Liquibase
- Bonnie Alvarado, Growth Marketing Programs Manager at LogMeIn
- Nina Church-Adams, Senior Director of Solution and Performance Marketing at Slalom
- Jen Nussinow Tasker, Director of Marketing and Communications at DSA Group
- Stephanie Bailey, VP of Revenue Marketing at Pendo.io
- Shreyansh Surana, Digital Marketing Program Manager at Microsoft
- Saneesh Veetil, Marketing Manager at Gramener
- Katy Martin, Product Marketing Manager at Lacework

CMOs

- Dirk Schart, CMO of RE'FLEKT
- James Gilbert, Head of Marketing at CRMNext
- Deanna Ransom, Global Head of Marketing and Marketing Services at Televerde
- Anthony Carignano, Technical Director of Marketing at Signite
- Kim Marie Ruquet, Consultant/Fractional CMO at Ruquet Advisors
- Michael McCunney, VP of Marketing at Revenue Analytics, Inc.

- Karien Pype, VP of Marketing at iText Software
- Clint Hughes, Consultant/Interim CMO/Governmental Liaison and Strategic Alliances at CH Revenue Consulting
- Allison Munro, CMO of Vena Solutions
- Jay Holden, Global Marketing Manager at Paul Mueller Company
- Lara Shackelford, CEO at TOSCA/X
- Ted Weyn, EVP of Systems Innovation, Marketing, Tele-Health and Government at Jackson and Coker
- Christine Seymour, CMO at Honeywell Connected Industrial
- Aby Varma, SVP of Marketing and Consumer Engagement at Hexagon AB
- Preeti Pande, CMO at Plug Power
- Gaurav Bhatia, CMO at PenFed Credit Union
- Caitlin Clark-Zigmond, Director of Global Demand Center and Mid-Market Marketing at Intuit
- Casey Cheshire, Founder and CMO of Cheshire Impact
- Mark Donnigan, Marketing and Business Growth Consultant at d-launch, LLC
- Darryl Praill, CRO at VanillaSoft
- Vince Koehler, VP of Marketing at Netsmart
- Mick Wilcox, CEO of Khronos
- Andy Mackensen, Co-founder and CMO of Caroo
- Helen Baptist, COO of PathFactory
- Matt Frisbie, CMO of Little Giant Ladder Systems
- Christine C. Davis, Principal of B2B Practice at Engagys LLC
- Rohit Prabhakar, Chief Growth Officer at EQ Holdings
- Shawn Herring, VP of Marketing at PandaDoc
- Denmark Francisco, CMO of Living Security

A CHARITABLE ENDEAVOR

One hundred percent of the proceeds of the first year of this book will go to New Story, an innovative nonprofit founded in 2015 that pioneers solutions to end global homelessness. Inspired to act after a trip to Haiti in 2013, CEO and co-founder Brett Hagler saw an opportunity to work with technology and transparency to challenge traditional methods of helping families meet their basic need for shelter.

New Story builds communities of $6,000–$10,000 homes in partnership with families living in extreme poverty. In four years, the nonprofit has funded over 2,300 homes, building twenty-two communities across Haiti, El Salvador, and Mexico and raising over $27 million to pioneer solutions through new software, processes, and homebuilding innovations.

In 2018, the organization partnered with ICON to create a first-of-its-kind machine to print the very first permitted 3D-printed home in North America. Then they took it even further: 3D-printing an entire community. It's no surprise that *Fast Company* recognized New Story as one of the world's most innovative companies in 2017 and as a top ten nonprofit in 2019.

One hundred percent of the donations to New Story go directly toward building communities. That includes the proceeds from this book, so we thank you for helping make dreams come true for deserving families.

Brett Hagler, CEO and co-founder of New Story, is a Y Combinator alum, 2016 *Forbes* "30 under 30" entrepreneur, author, speaker, and cancer survivor. He lives by the mantra, "It's only crazy until it's not," which is how he was able to go from starting a nonprofit at age twenty-five by building just one house to bringing breakthrough technologies to entire communities.

You can learn more about New Story at https://newstorycharity. org/.

PS For every review of this book (good or bad), we will put $10 toward this charity, so don't forget to write your review!

ACKNOWLEDGMENTS

ON ONE HAND, IT FEELS LIKE IT'S BEEN AN ETERNITY, and on the other hand, it feels like just yesterday since we started thinking about writing a book together. What made it so fun is that we didn't set about writing this book as the smartest people in the room. Instead, we were like kids wondering, asking questions, and listening to the best and brightest people in the world.

In many ways, this book was written by all of the people listed below. We want to thank each of you for your insights, wisdom, and inspiration that helped us make the book better and something we're proud to put our names on.

Thank you to:

Alex Symos, VP of GTM center of excellence at Edison Partners

Amber Bogie, ABM Manager/Strategy Owner at Degreed

Brian Halligan, CEO of HubSpot

Chris Lochhead, #1 Apple podcaster, #1 Amazon author, Category Designer, Co-creator of *Category Pirates* Newsletter

Craig Rosenberg, VP, Analyst at Gartner

Daniel Incandela, CMO at Terminus

Daniel Englebretson, Founder of Khronos

Jennifer Leaver, Sr. Marketing Manager, Demand Generation and Global ABM at Bazaarvoice

Jon Hallet, Executive Chairman of BetterCloud

Julie Brown, Global Director of Business Transformation— Services at Johnson Controls

Kelly Ford Buckley, General Partner and Fintech Investor at Edison Partners

Kevin O'Malley, VP, Account-Based Marketing at Gartner

Kristian Andersen, Partner at HighAlpha

Lindsay Cordell, VP, Enablement at Terminus

Mallory Lee, Revenue Operations at Terminus

Matt Belkin, EVP—Data, Strategy, and Partnerships at Terminus

Matt Howard, SVP, CMO at Sonatype

Manny Medina, CEO of Outreach

Mark Kosoglow, VP, Sales at Outreach

Mark Znutas, VP, GTM Strategy and Operations at HubSpot

Matt Howard, SVP, CMO at Sonatype

Max Altschuler, VP, Sales Engagement at Outreach

Meagen Eisenberg, CMO at TripActions

Nick Mehta, CEO at Gainsight

Ryan Ziglar, Partner at Edison Partners

Ryan Schwartz, SVP, Growth and Systems at TripActions

Scott Brinker, VP, Platform Ecosystem at HubSpot

Scott Dorsey, Managing Partner at HighAlpha

Sydney Sloan, CMO at SalesLoft

Tim Kopp, CEO at Terminus

Tim Satterwhite, CRO at Terminus

Nikki Morales, EA at Terminus

Justin Keller, VP of Brand at Terminus

Jeffrey Miller, Writer at Scribe Media

Todd Berkowitz, VP, Analyst at Gartner

Derek Schoettle, Partner at GreatHill Partners

Tim Hillson, CMO of EntryPont1

Dirk Schart, CMO of RE'FLEKT

Benjamin Pope, Marketing Automation and ABM Manager at Corevist

Paul Viviers, Founder of Social Insights Media

Lisa Pool, Owner of The Marketing Pool

Lauren Davis, Director of Marketing Operations at Funding U

Kate Hahn, Director of Global Demand Generation and Retention at Bazaarvoice

Seth Goldstein, Principal Creative Director at Goldstein Media, LLC

Gaurav Bhatia, CMO at PenFed Credit Union

Udayan Belsare, Europe Marketing Lead at Mphasis

Jay Holden, Global Marketing Manager at Paul Mueller Company

Joe Hader, Sr. Producer at Blue Cross and Blue Shield of Illinois, New Mexico, Montana, Oklahoma, and Texas

Vijay Damojipurapu, Founder and Principal Consultant of Stratyve

Brian Tripp, Client Partner at Accion Labs

Julian Parr, Sr. Marketing Manager at DLT Labs

Neha Pujari, Sr. Marketing Manager at BlazeClan Technologies

Tony Ramirez, VP of Economic Development at The Borderplex Alliance

Becky Hobbs, VP of Marketing at Brace

Lisa Sharapata, VP of Marketing—Brand and Demand at MindTickle

Sangeetha Mohan, Marketing Head at Mu Sigma Inc.

Ben Brook, Sr. Marketing Manager at SEO Travel

Kalim Aull, Co-founder of Servicecycle LLC

Wanda Dunaway, Regional Vice-President at Shaw Contract

Jessica Lalley, Founder of VoicesToConnect

Heather Robinette, freelance marketer

Karthiga Ratnam, CMO at Kingslake

Samir Kumar Sah, Founder and CEO of Pritbor

Stuart Winter-Tear, Director of Strategy and Solutions at
    ThreatModeler Software, Inc.

Michelle Waite, Marketing/Product Marketing at Skycatch

Kim Marie Ruquet, Consultant and Fractional CMO at Ruquet Advisors

Andy Mackensen, Co-founder and CMO of Caroo

Pablo Gonzalez, Co-founder, CMO, and Host of Chief Executive Connector
    Podcast *Be the Stage*

Himari Sawhney, Global Director of Demand Generation at Cellebrite

Dhriti Goyal, Head of Growth Marketing at Happay

Karthik Shankar, Sr. Program Manager at Amazon DSP

Natalia Bochan, Marketing and Technology Expert at nousEUROPA

Ted Weyn, EVP, Systems Innovation, Marketing, Tele-Health, and Government at Jackson and Coker

Allison Munro, CMO of Vena Solutions

Jen Leaver, Sr. Marketing Manager of Demand Generation and Global ABM at Bazaarvoice

Melissa Schaaf, Sr. Manager of Partner Marketing at Quantum Metric

Avnita Gulati, Sr. Director of Global Marketing Operations at Visa

Maneeza Aminy, CEO of Marvel Marketers

David Hoeller, Product Marketing Director at BlueVoyant

Erin Grubbs, Director of Marketing Programs at GoReact

Corrina Owens, Director of Marketing of ABM and Demand Generation at Profisee

Jimit Mehta, Head of ABM/Demand Generation at CommerceIQ

Alexander Caraballo, Data and Analytics Consultant at Retail, Healthcare, and Education at IPC Global

James Gilbert, Head of Marketing at CRMNext

Hema Deepak, Sr. Manager of Technical Marketing at Tejas Networks

Adam Hejna, Revenue Operations Leader at Kentico Kontent

Vipul Kalia of OnlineSales.ai

Clint Hughes, Consultant, Interim CMO, Chief Growth Officer, Governmental Liaison, and Strategic Alliances at CH Revenue Consulting

Barb Mosher Zinck, Content and Product Marketing Strategist at BMZ Content Strategies

Scott Marker, CEO and Founder at MSA^2 and Network In Action International franchise owner

ABOUT THE AUTHORS

SANGRAM VAJRE

SANGRAM RAN MARKETING AT PARDOT (WHICH WAS acquired by ExactTarget, and then ExactTarget was acquired by Salesforce for $2.7 billion). Soon after, Sangram co-founded Terminus, which recently ranked twenty-first in Deloitte's list of the fastest-growing companies and was named back-to-back as one of the best places to work.

On LinkedIn alone, Sangram has over 27,000 subscribers for his weekly *Becoming Intentional* newsletter and over 10 million views of his content in just the last two years. He has quickly become a GTM strategy expert and has been named one of the top twenty-one B2B marketing influencers in the world by the DMN network.

Sangram enjoys the learning experiences he receives from a private group of emerging CMOs and CMOs called the Peak Community, which hosts weekly sessions on getting 1 percent better each week.

He is the author of two books on marketing, a frequent keynote speaker, and a host of the top-fifty business podcast *Flip My Funnel* with over half a million downloads.

Sangram is an active member of the First Redeemer Church and lives in Atlanta with his wife, Manmeet, and two amazing kids, Krish and Kiara, who consistently remind him that he's got a big belly. ☺

BRYAN BROWN

BRYAN IS A SOFTWARE EXECUTIVE, SAAS PIONEER, and thought leader in the marketing and sales tech industry, both creating and bringing to market innovative software products and ideas, improving the way thousands of businesses grow and communicate with their customers. From co-founder to scale with multiple exits, he has the ability to envision and bring to life software in new categories both organically and through M&A.

At Terminus, Bryan led product and engineering as the company transitioned from an Account-Based Marketing ads product to an end-to-end Account-Based Engagement platform, and he now serves as chief strategy officer.

In the late 1990s/early 2000s, Bryan built Vtrenz. the first B2B marketing automation platform, which was fully multi-tenant and years ahead of the software-as-a-service movement, processing hundreds of millions of B2B buying signals, scoring leads, nurturing buyers, and alerting sales teams to their most important prospects.

Bryan married his sweetheart, Leah, in 1998. They have six children and have lived in Minnesota, Georgia, and Utah. They are passionate about family, faith, creativity, growth, mental health, empathy, being anxiously engaged in good causes, and the never-ending supply of new adventures that await them. Bryan accounts his many successes to his decision to put God first in his life.

In the mid-'90s, he had numerous life-changing experiences while serving as a missionary in Ireland. Since then, he has spent countless hours in leadership and youth ministry roles in his church and community.

For all templates, assessments and bonus material mentioned in the book, go to https://www.themovebook.com/or scan this:

Oh! And yes, we are also releasing a documentary. It's called *The 7 Truths and One Lie*.

We interviewed some of the best GTM leaders, operations, and pioneers over the last few decades to compile a once in a lifetime must-watch documentary.

Why?

Because GTM is hard and complicated and confusing.

To help you plot your next **MOVE**, we created a video companion examining what go to market (GTM) means in a post-pandemic, tech obsessed, algorithm driven, unnecessarily complex world of business to business sales and marketing.

In a choose your own adventure approach, you can watch our documentary in one sitting or experience it through seven episodes featuring category creators, innovators, and pioneers in b2b tech. Sangram takes you on a journey, taking the six truths into action while unveiling the one thing you're likely getting wrong. Along the way, gain access to the templates, scorecard, and other resources mentioned in the book, taking your GTM approach to the next level.

Simply go to https://www.themovebook.com/ and find your next **MOVE**.

CPSIA information can be obtained
at www.ICGtesting.com
Printed in the USA
JSHW021036010322
23445JS00002B/7

9 781544 523378